Plato's Progeny

CLASSICAL INTER/FACES

Also available

Lucretius and the Modern World
W.R. Johnson

Translating Words, Translating Cultures
Lorna Hardwick

PLATO'S PROGENY

How Socrates and Plato Still Captivate the Modern Mind

Melissa Lane

Duckworth

First published in 2001 by
Gerald Duckworth & Co. Ltd.
61 Frith Street, London W1D 3JL
Tel: 020 7434 4242
Fax: 020 7434 4420
Email: enquiries@duckworth-publishers.co.uk
www.ducknet.co.uk

A catalogue record for this book is available
from the British Library

ISBN 0 7156 2892 5

Typeset by Ray Davies
Printed in Great Britain by
Biddles Limited, *www.biddles.co.uk*

Contents

Note on References
and Bibliography

Because this book is designed for the general reader, works are cited
in foreign languages only where I know of no adequate translation
or for the sake of acknowledging a standard edition. Quotations are
from published translations wherever possible. Where a work is
referred to by a foreign language title, translation from it is my own
unless otherwise stated. Space restraints in this series mean that,
while full references are given in the notes, only a select number of
works are listed as further reading, and that little if any secondary
literature on the authors discussed could be noted. A fuller biblio-
graphy and other further information can be found at:
http://www.kings.cam.ac.uk/histecon/plato/index.htm.

Ancient texts are cited by the conventional numbering system (by
section and/or line number) in each case. For ancient authors other
than Plato and Aristotle, Loeb editions have been used. For Aristotle, the standard Greek edition is the Oxford text, and the
translation is that of *The Complete Works of Aristotle: the revised
Oxford translation*, 2 vols, edited by J. Barnes (Princeton, 1984). For
Plato, the Greek edition is the Oxford text, and the translations are
those in the new standard collection, *Plato: Complete Works*, edited
with Introduction and Notes by J.M. Cooper, with associate editor
D.S. Hutchison (Hackett, 1997). The works included in that volume
are as follows, in alphabetical order:

*Alcibiades**, Second Alcibiades*, Apology, Axiochus*, Charmides,
Clitophon**, Cratylus, Critias, Crito, Definitions*, Demodocus*,
Epigrams***, Epinomis*, Eryxias*, Euthydemus, Euthyphro, Gor-
gias, Halcyon*, Hipparchus*, Greater Hippias*, Lesser Hippias, Ion,
On Justice*, Laches, Laws, Letters***, Lysis, Menexenus, Meno,*

Minos*, Parmenides, Phaedo, Philebus, Protagoras, Republic, Rival Lovers*, Sisyphos*, Sophist, Statesman, Symposium, Theages*, Theaetetus, Timaeus, On Virtue*

* 'It is generally agreed by scholars that Plato is not the author of this work.'

** 'It is not generally agreed by scholars whether Plato is the author of this work.'

*** As to Plato's authorship of the individual Letters and Epigrams, consult the respective introductory notes in Cooper, *Plato*. (The attributions quoted are from Cooper, *Plato*, p. vi.)

Of those dialogues whose authenticity is not in question, Socrates appears in a major or minor part in all except the *Laws*.

The works of Xenophon in which Socrates is mentioned are as follows: *Anabasis, Hellenica, Memorabilia, Symposium*. Those of Aristophanes are *Birds*, *Clouds* and *Frogs*.

*

Author's note

A brief comment on how this book compares to others in recent literature, all listed in Further Reading and referenced in the Notes. A.T. Peperzak and C. Zuckert (for Plato), S. Kofman and A. Nehamas (for Socrates) have each provided compelling overviews of the readings of Plato and Socrates respectively by important figures in what might broadly be considered postmodernism – collectively including Derrida, Gadamer, Heidegger, Levinas, Nietzsche and Strauss – as well as Montaigne, Hegel and Kierkegaard. None of them, however, has sought to put the postmodern preoccupation with Plato into any broader historical contexts, as is attempted here.

Acknowledgements

This book was inspired by a paper given by Myles Burnyeat (cited in the Conclusion), who explored the new nineteenth-century interest in the *Republic* and concluded that there was a book on the modern reception of Plato waiting to be written. He has pursued the idea in several important papers, particularly about the Victorians; I hope this further elaboration does it justice.

For comments on earlier drafts, bibliographical advice, discussion, or all of the above, I wish to thank: Deborah Blake (Duckworth), Susanna Morton Braund, Myles Burnyeat, Paul Cartledge, Edward Castleton, Verity Harte, Douglas Hedley, Christian Illies, Susan James, Robert Kargman, Norman Lane, Sheila Lane, Douglas Moggach, Eric Nelson, George Pattison, Michael O'Brien, Emma Rothschild, Malcolm Schofield, Jonathan Scott, Ben Shaw, Michael Sonenscher, and especially, for many crucial and instructive conversations, Emile Perreau-Saussine and Martin Ruehl. Audiences at the Cambridge Seminar in the History of Philosophy, the Cambridge International Summer School in History, and the Institute of Historical Research Seminar in the History of Ideas, queried earlier versions. The staffs of the British Library, Classics Faculty Library at Cambridge (in particular Librarian Dr Judith Waring), Cambridge University Library, Modern Archives Centre of King's College Cambridge (in particular Archivist Ros Moad), Library of the Warburg Institute, and Wren Library of Trinity College Cambridge all deserve warm thanks.

Nick and Sarah Ray kindly volunteered the use of their cottage in Wales at just the right moment for writing. The Brownsteins, the Cambridge Kargmans, the Lanes, and the Malins all gave succour at a point of rest. Rosie Peppin Vaughan and David Price provided vital editorial assistance in the final stages. Throughout, Andrew

Lovett cooked innumerable meals in the intervals of his own composing. Without his loving encouragement the book would never have been finished.

Three of the 'elders' to whom my previous book was dedicated have passed away since that was published: Zdenek Hrdlicka, a scholar, statesman, and sometime dissident; Gabriela Rodriguez Loria, an uncommon spirit, who loved justice, beauty and friendship; and my grandmother Sally Kargman Shelist Perlow, teacher and dancer extraordinaire. I dedicate this book in love to their memories, and to the presence of two of the other important elders in my life: Max and Marie Kargman, who were thinking seriously about Socrates long before I was.

King's College Cambridge   Melissa Lane
1 February 2001

1

Introduction

> We run very fast, but there is this horrible Plato, at the end of
> the course, still abreast of us. Our novelties we can find all in
> his book. He has anticipated our latest neology.
>
> Ralph Waldo Emerson, *Journals* (1850)

Did Plato condemn homosexuality? In 1993, defending a state
constitutional amendment which excluded homosexuals from
anti-discrimination laws, the state of Colorado argued that he had.
The claim that Plato held homosexuality to be a threat to public
morals was made to bolster the state's case that its new constitutional provision was well founded. Scholars from Harvard, Oxford
and Princeton testified in support of the state, while a scholar from
Brown University was called in to testify against.[1]

To find Plato at the centre of debate in a contemporary courtroom
is astonishing enough. What is further remarkable is that for centuries Plato had been roundly excoriated, or avidly read, for exactly
the opposite reason: as a lover and admirer of same-sex relationships. Renaissance monks attacked him for perverting his
associates; Victorian students were inflamed by schoolboy study of
Plato in Greek, and incensed by expurgated or vague translations;
a Cambridge don composed his own Platonic dialogue explaining
homoeroticism as a natural longing of some souls.[2] 'Platonic love'
has come to mean any intense non-sexual relationship, but its
earlier meaning was that of homoerotic relationships that might not
be sexually consummated, but were filled with passion and spiritual
intensity.

The immediate reason that Plato could be claimed both for the
prosecution and for the defence in Colorado is a banal one: the two
sides emphasized different parts of his writing, all of which must be

1

understood against the background of Athenian practices of homo-erotic relationships between men and youths. The *Laws*, Plato's last work, criticizes these practices, proposing that male same-sex relationships be punished, while also placing severe restrictions even on marriage. On the other hand, in the *Symposium*, his luminous portrait of Socrates, Aristophanes, Alcibiades and others discoursing on love, Plato has Socrates recount, in the words of a priestess, the way a man's love for a beautiful youth can set him on the ascent towards love of what is beautiful in itself. One might say that this is just a matter of a writer not knowing his own mind, or toying with the luxury of writing dialogues rather than ever speaking in his own voice, or growing more conservative as he aged. But such points do not address the gravitational pull exercised by Plato in the Colorado case, as on so many other aspects of contemporary culture. Of all the illustrious ranks of philosophers ancient and modern, Plato has become the undisputed champion, and in the Colorado trial his endorsement was the supreme prize.

Consider some summary positions taken by prominent modern thinkers, each ascribing to Plato the fundamental goods or ills of modern thought.

- All of Western philosophy consists of 'footnotes to Plato'.[3] (A.N. Whitehead)
- Plato perverted and distorted the subsequent course of Western philosophy. (Friedrich Nietzsche)
- Plato's *Republic* shows him as the greatest political idealist. (Hermann Cohen)
- Plato's *Republic* proves that he was the first totalitarian. (Karl Popper)
- Plato was Socrates' most faithful pupil. (Benjamin Jowett)
- Plato betrayed his teacher Socrates: 'it is Socrates, not Plato, whom we need.' (R.H.S. Crossman)

The point is not only that Plato has excited both admiration and hostility. It is that each particular pairing – Plato as founder and as corrupter of metaphysics, Plato as idealist and as totalitarian, Plato as faithful or traitorous to Socrates – constitutes a characteristically

2

modern debate. The first could be said to constitute the intellectual history of postmodernism. The second spans the tensions of the Cold War. Together they give rise inexorably to the third. For in pondering Plato's posthumous guilt for the destructiveness of the twentieth century, one cannot but ask, was Plato continuing, or betraying, the legacy of his teacher Socrates?

What follow here are three interconnected essays on these themes, exploring the intellectual history of the ways in which Plato and Socrates have been read. The focus is on the nineteenth and twentieth centuries, shown to be distinctive against selected backdrops of earlier readings. Thus the earlier readings of Plato's sympathy with homoerotic love throw the Colorado controversy, in which the state invoked Plato as an unimpeachable and honoured moral authority for current public values, into sharp, and strange, relief. In a book of this length no single figure can be treated in the contextual depth that intellectual history would normally demand, nor can the scope be comprehensive (an impossible task anyway). I hope instead to make a contribution in the importance of the questions asked, the diversity of the evidence studied, and the quality of the arguments deployed.[4]

A brief survey of these arguments may prove useful here. Chapter 2 confronts the question of the relation between Plato and Socrates. Socrates wrote nothing, and the modern presumption is that we know him best from his appearance as protagonist of most of Plato's writings (we shall see in Chapter 2 just why this might be thought presumptuous). The argument here is that the ancients and moderns share a civic reading of Socrates, which in the ancient world was specifically political – in terms of his democratic impact – to which the moderns have added a concern with his impact on the Greek culture of his day. Alongside these two kinds of civic readings have flourished ethical and religious interpretations: Socrates as martyr and as sage. The civic focus of modern readers has sometimes frozen Socrates in relation to the city, cutting off any understanding of the broader ethical and religious questions. Modern thinkers who have found most to learn from Socrates have combined the civic and the ethical: not simply ranging him for or against the city, but asking what the ethical and personal implications of citizenship for an individual might be. The questions raised in this chapter include: Why was Socrates killed? Was he innocent or guilty, an oligarch or a recluse, devoted to reason or to piety? Socrates immortalized himself by drinking hemlock at the orders of the Athenian democracy: he made himself the first martyr to philosophy, the most famous casualty of the war between philosophy and the city. Did he mean his life, or his death, to lead to that fate?

These political questions recur in a different form in Chapter 4, where the modern controversy over Plato's politics is considered. But first we must meet the modern controversy over his philosophy: the charges that he introduced a malign dualism (postulating an ultimate reality beyond the sensible world) and a malign foundationalism (purporting to found ethical truth upon that ultimate reality) which together have distorted the course of philosophy ever since. These charges can be summarized as the 'postmodern' challenge to Plato, though to escape the many ambiguities of this description, I prefer the term 'post-Nietzschean' in what follows. Chapter 3 examines readings of Plato which stand up against each count: readings which find ultimate reality immanent in the sensible world, and which make ethics depend on aspiration rather than simply on metaphysical foundation. The upshot is that Plato's ethics can be interpreted not as the bane of Western philosophy but as remarkably similar to the self-fashioning which post-Nietzscheans recommend.

While Chapters 2 and 4 are linked by their political themes, Chapters 3 and 4 have in common the astonishing venom unleashed against Plato in the twentieth century: against his philosophy (Chapter 3) and against his politics (Chapter 4). Just why Plato has attracted such attacks will be considered below and again in the Conclusion. In Chapter 4, the political controversy is shown to centre on the strange way Plato uses radical measures to embed a commitment to hierarchy into his holistic vision of politics. To liberals, his holism has looked reactionary, but the measures prescribed in the *Republic* for achieving this holism – including communism of property and procreation among the ruling elite – have looked dangerously radical to many. Was Plato a communist?

4

1. Introduction

Was he a totalitarian? Was he a utopian? Is the *Republic* (the text which has become central for modern readers of Plato) a programme for political domination, an idle fantasy, or a summons to education? The argument in Chapter 4 is parallel to that of Chapter 2: that these controversies over Plato's politics, by setting him in one ideological mould or another, have missed the possibility of learning from him. What Plato's political writings have to teach involves the interconnection of themes – education and legislation, democracy and culture, liberty and self-discipline – which modern controversies have kept too rigidly apart.

The survey of modern readings of Plato and Socrates in each chapter is a critical one: in each, a case for one reading over others emerges. That political ideology needs to consider broader questions of culture and ethics is the common theme of Chapers 2 and 4; that ethics, in turn, can in practice be freed from its metaphysical foundations and found in the intersection of art, love and beauty, is the theme of Chapter 3. Emerging from reflections on history, the readings recommended here are of course historically embedded themselves. They begin from the centrality of the *Republic*, now taken for granted, and work outwards to the other dialogues. They consider a Plato freed from the full sway of Neoplatonic or Christian dogma, but find riches to be recovered from each of those earlier contexts. They attend primarily to Plato's dialogues, not his letters. The Plato advocated in the arguments running through the book is not the only possible Plato. It is a partial Plato, focusing on certain themes and dialogues. Nevertheless, as cousin to certain great tribes and generations of Platos introduced in this book, the Plato advocated here enjoys a large number of important family resemblances. More important still, he is a Plato for the twenty-first century, born of reflection on the great age of ideologies (1789-1989: from the storming of the Bastille to the collapse of the Berlin Wall) in order to point a path beyond them.

The cast of characters consists of writers, philosophers and poets. There is little to be said here of the history of Platonic scholarship narrowly conceived, or the history of translation. (Three influential translations can be briefly contrasted: the Neoplatonic translation into English by Thomas Taylor [1804]; the Romantic translation into

German by Friedrich Schleiermacher [1804-28]; and the idealist translation into French by Victor Cousin [1822-40], each with rival predecessors and successors in its own tongue.) The cast is primarily though not exclusively English- and German-speaking, including Americans and Austrians in its ranks. I focus on Anglophone and Germanophone writers partly for the sake of coherence, and partly because contrasts between dominant approaches in each of these contexts emerged over the course of the nineteenth century. These contrasts culminated in the first half of the twentieth century, when influential English writers attacked Plato as a totalitarian, while some of their German counterparts invoked him instead as a heroic political leader and civic educator.

To stylize this as an English-German confrontation would be far too simple. On the one hand, the two traditions constantly cross-fertilized, as in Arnaldo Momigliano's observation that 'all the German studies on Greek history of the last fifty years of the nineteenth century are either for or against [the English historian, George] Grote'.[5] On the other hand, writers native to each country went against the trends described above; the Austrian Karl Popper, writing in English in New Zealand, would have to count as an honorary Anglo-American for his pro-Socrates, anti-Plato stance. Still, the attacks made by English writers on German readings of Plato and vice versa in the first half of the twentieth century indicate a real divergence among dominant figures at that point, and keeping the focus on writers from these two contexts helps to identify and explain what was at stake.

A number of the figures presented here will be familiar to readers with certain interests. Some (for example, Victorian readers of Plato; Nietzsche's view of Socrates) have been exceptionally well studied by specialists. Others, however, (for example, the George Circle writers on Plato and their influence) are far less familiar. This juxtaposition of new and familiar figures, together with the lines of argument used to connect them, should make the book instructive for readers with specialized and general interests in the subject alike.

Those, then, are the arguments as to 'how' Plato and Socrates have captivated the modern mind. We turn now to sketch three reasons 'why'. The first, the (laboured and difficult) rebirth of democracy as a political ideal in the eighteenth and nineteenth centuries, attached to the 'modernity' of the French Revolution, will be considered at length in the second and fourth chapters. The second is the modern preoccupation with the origins and authority of faith, and in particular with the public authority of Christianity in Europe. Having played a crucial role in the early Church, Platonism was drawn upon once again to bolster, or sometimes to supplant, Christian faith (in particular, this time, Protestant denominations) in the nineteenth century. This was particularly true in Britain, but it also characterizes the incorporation of Christianity in the great German systems of philosophical idealism. Modern attacks on the validity of religon and of metaphysics often fastened on the quasi-religious readings of Plato which had turned his thought into a supplement or substitute for Christian faith.

These two arguments have a common feature, in that the problematics unleashed by democratic pressures and religious preoccupations were not addressed by recourse to Plato alone. In Britain, the lionization of Plato belongs within a context of Victorian preference for Greece over Rome within the further context of the general role of the classics in providing a bond 'of intellectual communion among civilized men'.[6] The preference for Greece has been argued to derive from two discontinuities – one political, the other religious – which the Victorians felt separated them from the previously dominant image of the Romans. Politically, models of the Roman republic appeared less relevant to the rise of democracy than Athens, the place where democracy had been invented; religiously, the purely pagan Greeks were paradoxically more appealing as models or supplements to Christian faith than the Romans – who had, after all, in the decadent imperial age, persecuted the first Christians.

Plato, then, was not the only Greek to be celebrated by the Victorians. Gladstone was an authority on Homer, whose pure warrior spirit and heroic morality exercised widespread appeal; the tragic poets were also revived, as was the historian Thucydides. Most relevant to the status of Plato however is the simultaneous revival of interest in Aristotle. Described by Dante as 'the master of those who know', Aristotle had been simply 'the philosopher' for centuries during which Plato enthusiasts were relatively few and less institutionally entrenched in the universities. In the nineteenth and twentieth centuries – my main focus – Aristotle's emphasis on the substantial union of form and matter, and his vision of equal citizenship and political participation, inspired philosophers to use him as a model against Plato's perceived failings. In broad terms, if Plato was attacked as the villain of twentieth-century philosophy, Aristotle emerged as its hero, with Socrates as an ambiguous third: Plato as the pernicious idealist and imposer of tyranny, Aristotle as the sane pragmatist and defender of community, and Socrates as the model of the free (but possibly politically inimical) individual.

Yet it was Plato, not Aristotle, on whom attention fastened most keenly in the Colorado search for political legitimacy. And if one were to ask the proverbial passenger on the Clapham omnibus to name the greatest philosopher, it would almost certainly be Plato rather than Aristotle who would spring to mind. Where Protestantism predominates in Britain and America, this would be partly for the local reason that Aristotle was too implicated in the theology of Rome to serve as a model for troubled Anglicans or dissenting intellectuals. But the more fundamental reason lies in the third explanation for the predominance of Plato: the modern preoccupation with origins.

Two senses combine in this preoccupation, and as we shall see, at least two divergent attitudes have been spawned by it. The first sense is again a religious one: originality in the sense of faithfulness to the origin, a function of Lutheran literalism about the Bible which was transferred to Plato in the nineteenth century.[7] And second was the Romantic idea of genius, which flattened out the weight of the philosophical tradition just as Luther flattened out the hierarchy and interpretative tradition of the Church. Revelation became a function of the original text as met by the mind of the reader, unmediated by anything that had passed in the centuries between.[8]

Together these influences worked to elevate Plato above Aristotle and also Cicero, who for centuries had been more central to philosophical education. Both Aristotle and Cicero had been heavily mediated by the philosophical traditions which grew up in their name, Aristotle as synthesized by the scholastics, Cicero as an eclectic sceptic and the voice of republican Rome. Recovered piecemeal in the Latin West, in translations from Arabic and Greek, Plato was read by the educated few and worshipped by a handful of enthusiasts. But his work was marginal to the great syntheses of the Middle Ages and Renaissance; it therefore evaded the brunt of the attacks on Aristotle which inaugurated the early modern age of science.

Yet if Plato had been marginal in one sense, in another he was fundamental. He was, after all, Aristotle's teacher and a key source for Ciceronian Rome and Augustinian Christianity. And this status made him a magnet in the search for originality – both as the beginning and as the inspired genius. At this point, however, the two divergent attitudes came into play. On the one hand was the attitude that the moderns should imitate the ancients. As the eighteenth-century German enthusiast for Greek art, J.J. Winckelmann, influentially wrote: 'There is but one way for the moderns to become great, and perhaps unequalled; I mean, by imitating the ancients.'[9] On the other hand, in philosophy the ambition came to be not simply to imitate the ancients, but to surpass them (Kant's role in this will be explained in Chapter 3). This is how Plato was installed at the pinnacle of the Western tradition, becoming both the source *par excellence*, and the standard to be surpassed. This also explains the irresoluble modern preoccupation with the relation between Socrates and Plato: for if Plato is made the prime source, what of his teacher? It is characteristically modern to seek an unimpeachable moral source and then immediately try to impeach it. The paradoxical modern longing to be both authentic and new is at the heart of why Plato and Socrates have so captivated the modern mind.

The 'we' of this book – the 'we' who are captivated by Plato and Socrates – are manifold. 'We' the literate philosophical and political culture of Europe and America – yes – but also 'we' of circles in Buenos Aires, Moscow, Somalia, Tokyo, Teheran – all places where Plato has been read and discussed in recent years. 'We' philosophers, but also 'we' artists, poets, clerics, feminists, labourers – all characters who will figure in the pages to come. Even 'we' the Vulcans of

Star Trek: a 'Voyager' programme features a book called 'A Cave Beyond Logic: Vulcan Perspectives on Platonic Thought'. Plato, and the question of Plato's relation to Socrates, seem to offer something which we need, which we can't stop thinking about, which is fundamental to our understanding of our modern selves. This book is an invitation to reflect on this striking feature of our reflections. Why think about Plato and Socrates today? The immediate question is not whether we should (on which see the Conclusion). It is why, and how, we do.

2

Who Was Socrates?

Our wants are the same as those which made Socrates ... [say, that] he, or any man who held the same course as to current clap-trap that he did, was 'the only true politician of men now living'.

> Matthew Arnold, *God and the Bible* (1875),
> quoting freely from Plato's *Gorgias*

... the victory of Socrates over Callicles is not an academic question, it is a question of the life and death of modern civilization.

> George F. Thomas, *Spirit and Its Freedom* (1939), on
> the confrontation between Socrates and the sophist
> Callicles portrayed in the same dialogue

We have all killed [Socrates]. This is not by not following, but by fleeing him, him and his destiny, by having invented philosophy, politics, political philosophy, servants which have mastered man who degrades and hollows them; by having reduced Thought to science ...

> Maurice Clavel, *Nous l'avons tous tué
> ou 'ce juif de Socrate!* ...' (1977)

Introduction

An elitist Victorian, battling the conformism of mass culture. An earnest Christian communitarian, girding America for the defence of democracy against fascism. A French onetime Maoist, scarred by the aftermath of the 1968 student revolts to the point of becoming a Catholic. What do they have in common? – all appealed to Socrates

11

as the model for their civic stance. Following Plato's *Apology*, the Victorian, Arnold, saw Socrates as a gadfly, who could sting complacent Englishmen into greater awareness of their limitations. Reading Socrates as a more straightforward moralist, the American, Thomas, sought in his philosophy a foundation for democratic politics (despite Socrates' own, at the very least, difficult relations with the Athenian democracy). And standing in the line of those who hold that there was more to Socrates than realized by any image or creed, the Frenchman Clavel invoked him as a symbol of the value of independent thought, always exceeding the claims of any moral system or political regime. For them all, Socrates' civic stance – whether narrowly democratic or more broadly cultural – is exemplary for the modern citizen, a stance which, by invoking Socrates, they thereby claim as their own.

Who was the man who could appeal to such diverse followers? Born to a humble artisan family, Socrates attracted a circle of prominent disciples, with whom he pursued the question of how to live well rather than simply succeed in gaining power and influence at all costs. Stories sprang up about Socrates. His conversations with all comers in search of knowledge, on the grounds that 'the unexamined life is not worth living' (*Apology* 38a); his insistence that the health of the soul and the pursuit of virtue should be the aims of individuals and of politicians, in place of the pursuit of wealth, power, and glory; his remarkably ugly face, which concealed the beauty of his soul in a way repellent and fascinating to the beauty-loving Greeks; his legendary self-control, which enabled him to stand outside for hours in the cold while meditating on philosophy; his rejection of the commitment to retaliation which was central to Greek ethics: these are among the characteristics ascribed to him by his closest disciples.

But the life of Socrates might never have become so resonant were it not for the manner of his death. Indicted in 399 BCE at the age of seventy on the charges of neglecting Athens' gods, introducing new gods and corrupting the youth, Socrates was tried before a democratic jury, convicted and sentenced to death. When ordered, he obediently drank a cup of poisonous hemlock and died calm and cheerful to the last, having declared that he did not fear death since he could not know it to be an evil (*Apology* 29a). The meaning of his life and death – recounted in the testimony of his friends and enemies, and embroidered by later legends – has posed an enigmatic challenge to every generation since.

The fact that Socrates lived in and died at the behest of democratic Athens (the pre-eminent democracy of the ancient world) might seem self-evidently to raise the question of Socrates' relation to his city: his relation to its democracy and his relation to its culture. And indeed, none of the modern invocations quoted above could ignore these two dimensions of what we may call the civic question. But the image of an *engagé* Socrates, who either served or harmed the democratic regime and the cultural values of his native city, went into eclipse between the fall of democracy in Athens some seventy years after Socrates' death, and the age of enlightenment and revolution symbolized by the dates 1776 and 1789. In the centuries between, when most thinkers were hostile to what Athens had represented and sure that it had been wrong in putting Socrates to death, the overwhelming tendency was to see Socrates not in civic but in ethical and religious terms.

For some, these terms were straightforwardly positive. For the Stoics, as later many others, including the French priest Fénelon who was tutor to the grandson of Louis XIV, Socrates was venerated as a wise and virtuous sage. And for Seneca, as later for Alexander Pope, the virtue displayed in Socrates' calm and cheerful death was a model to be followed in his own death. But others were puzzled by a paradox in Plato's writings. In the *Apology* (21a-23b) Socrates reports the discovery that he, like everyone else he has questioned in response to the Delphic oracle's pronouncement that no one was wiser than he, in fact knows nothing: all are equally lacking in wisdom. But in the *Meno* and other dialogues, he defends the view that virtue requires knowledge. It should follow that, lacking knowledge, Socrates could not have been virtuous. Yet the third leg of the paradox is that both Plato and Xenophon present him as having been supremely virtuous: perfectly courageous in war; perfectly temperate in physical pleasures; perfectly just in his obedience to his own death sentence. Speculation about this paradox – as to whether Socrates was simply naturally wise (Montaigne) or rationally knowledgeable to the point of obnoxious pedantry (the courtiers of Louis XIV), whether he was virtuous out of ignorance (Rousseau) or out of knowledge (Diderot) – became acute during Enlightenment debates about the value of reason and its moral consequences.

The question whether Socrates was wise and virtuous also bore heavily on the question of his piety, which was vexed by the fact that he had lived in a pagan age, before the revelation of Christ. To maintain that Socrates had been perfectly virtuous, an early Christian such as Justin Martyr had to insist that he had already been inspired by the divine word. Others denied that Socrates or any pagan could have been perfectly virtuous without Christian revelation. The choice then was between admiring him as having prefigured Christ in suffering a parallel martyrdom, and disparaging him as having been opposed to Christ by reason of his own deficiencies. A further complication in evaluating Socratic piety is that Plato reports him as appealing at crucial moments to a *daimonion* or tutelary spirit, which in the *Apology* and *Crito*, for example, is said to have warned him when he was about to do anything wrong. Whether the *daimonion* was a form of divine revelation, the voice of Socrates' inner conscience, or simply (as Nietzsche speculated) an ear infection, its interpretation embarrassed those who wished to see Socrates as a pure rationalist.

These sometimes vitriolic debates about the ethical-religious significance of Socrates continue to preoccupy at least some modern thinkers. But central to modern thought about Socrates has been the revival of the ancient conundrum as to whether Socrates was for or against democracy in Athens. And this democratic theme has been accompanied by a second and new theme in the civic evaluation of Socrates: the question of his historical significance for the evolution of Greek culture.

The continuous fascination which Socrates has exercised over Western culture is thus marked by two major discontinuities. On the one hand, a long hiatus between the ancients and the moderns who have bestirred themselves concerning Socrates the democrat or anti-democrat. On the other hand, the modern invention of historical method and historical perspective, which has added to the evaluation of Socrates' civic stance a new concern with his cultural impact. Some moderns, considering Athens as a parallel to their own state, have condemned the Athenians for killing Socrates on the grounds that he was a true democrat; others have vindicated them. Others still, seeing Athens as historically situated in a doomed pre-Christian world, have argued that by Athenian lights the death of Socrates may have been justified, even though Socrates' challenge to democratic culture was valid.

These two modern tendencies have sometimes undermined one another: 'Socrates' as a democratic icon for the present day sits ill with 'Socrates' the ancient Greek to be assigned his proper place in history. I will argue that the democratic readings tend to over-simplify Socrates' philosophy and politics, making him a frozen icon of individual dissent. On the other hand, the cultural-historical readings cannot account for the very iconic status which they none-theless bestow upon him. Syntheses have appeared, which combine these perspectives together with the older ethical-religious con-cerns, and these will be examined in a later part of the chapter. As the quotations from Arnold, Thomas and Clavel suggest, all of these great themes – the individual in relation to society, philosophy in relation to democracy and culture, and the question for each individ-ual of how to live and die – are themes which Socrates inescapably symbolizes for the modern age and which reflecting on him can help us to understand.

The dual modern concerns with the civic Socrates – an ancient democratic one, and a novel cultural-historical one – have been pressed upon us in these forms:

- Was Athens right or wrong to convict Socrates?
- Did he mean to uphold Athenian democracy or to undermine it?
- Was Socratic philosophy the salvation or the subversion of Greek culture?

But before turning to this agenda, there is a prior question to be addressed, itself a characteristic product of the modern concern with historical methods. The sketches of Socrates given above drew heavily on the writings of Plato, which are seen today as the obvious and sometimes only reliable source for the image of Socrates. But the very process which has made Plato central has also thrown up fundamental questions about just how much Plato can tell us about Socrates. So we begin by addressing the issue of our knowledge of Socrates, which hinges on these explosive historical questions:

- Did any of Plato's writings portray Socrates accurately?
- Did Plato, anywhere in his writings, betray the values for which the real Socrates had stood?

If Socrates wrote nothing, how can we know anything about him?

Socrates wrote nothing. It is indisputable that he lived, yet all that we know of him comes from the testimony of others. In 423 BCE, twenty-four years before his trial, the comic poet Aristophanes made him the central figure in his play *Clouds*: here Socrates was portrayed as one of the many sophistic teachers who crowded Athens, atypical only in being as interested in useless knowledge as in the kind of knowledge that could earn his students political power. Aristophanes also alluded to him in other plays, while in the wake of Socrates' death, writing about him became a popular ancient literary genre. Among the contributions which survive are the biographies written centuries later by Diogenes Laertius and by Plutarch, who along with Cicero reported some of the many legends surrounding him.

Of all the dialogues and memoirs of Socrates written after his death, the most extensive and most important are those of his associates, Plato and Xenophon. Plato was an aristocratic young Athenian, who would later recall (if his *Seventh Letter* is accepted as authentic) that upon meeting Socrates he gave up his political and literary ambitions to dedicate himself to philosophy; Xenophon was an Athenian general who was in exile at the time of Socrates' trial and wrote his memoirs abroad. Both wrote versions of the *Apology* (from the Greek *apologia*, meaning 'defence speech') given by Socrates at his trial. Both also wrote versions of symposia (drinking parties) at which Socrates was purportedly present, though with different guest lists. Xenophon's *Memorabilia* and *Oeconomicus*

recount a number of fragmentary Socratic conversations and anec-
dotes about the great man, while Socrates appears as a major or a
minor character in all Plato's dialogues other than the *Laws*. Plato
himself never appears as a character in his own writings, though his
characters report him as present during the trial and absent from
Socrates' actual death.

In the ancient world, all the major philosophical schools (Stoics,
Cynics and Academic Sceptics) appealed to Socrates as a model,
interpreting the legends and stories about his life as best suited
their own particular slant. But from the Renaissance onwards, as
scholars began to be concerned about the fact that they had inherited diverse and sometimes contradictory accounts of Socrates,
Xenophon tended to be preferred as a source of stories about Socrates as he 'really was'. This was largely because of the apparent
plainness of his style compared with Plato's baroque literary concoc-
tions. As a philosopher himself, Plato was suspected of having put
his own views into the mouth of his character 'Socrates', whereas the
upright old soldier Xenophon was assumed to be reliably straightforward in his accounts. In his writings, Xenophon sought to prove
that Socrates was useful and beneficial to the city, encouraging all
his interlocutors to pursue virtue. The darker or at least shadier
sides of Plato's Socrates, his irony and paradoxes, seem to be absent
from Xenophon.

The eighteenth century saw a number of attempts to clarify what
could be securely known of Socrates by collating and comparing the
sources. These culminated in the systematic inquiries of Friedrich
Schleiermacher, who is credited with the elaboration of source-
criticism. Schleiermacher plumped for neither Plato nor Xenophon
outright. Instead he tried to triangulate between them. His interpretative rule or 'canon' was to inquire as follows:

What may Socrates have been, over and above what Xenophon
has described, without however contradicting the strokes of
character, and the practical maxims, which Xenophon dis-
tinctly delivers as those of Socrates: and what must he have
been, to give Plato a right, and an inducement, to exhibit him
as he has done in his dialogues?[1]

Schleiermacher's canon implies that none of the 'Socrateses' whom we meet in the ancient texts depicts the man exactly as he was, although the historian may be able to reconstruct him using clues from all of them. Not all scholars have accepted this rule, but the clear statement of the problem raised new questions which have been pursued ever since. It was hoped that by using source-criticism, the views of Socrates could be independently identified and so separated out from the Platonic dialogues, leaving the remainder as what Plato meant to say in his own voice. This hope was bolstered by the manifest differences in style and in the arguments put forward by the 'Socrates' character in different Platonic dialogues. Perhaps, it was thought, some dialogues present Plato's view of the 'real' Socrates, while others use 'Socrates' as a mouthpiece for Plato's own views. And perhaps new methods of textual criticism could explain the order of the dialogues in such a way as to make the meaning of these changing manifestations of Socrates clear. Then one might hope to establish a well-grounded account of who both Socrates and Plato were, in terms of what they believed.

Such an aim was not merely antiquarian. Its adoption had two important consequences. On the one hand, whereas Schleiermacher's canon had addressed itself equally to Plato and Xenophon, the hope of securing distinct portraits of Socrates and Plato from within Plato's writings alone would eventually take on a life of its own. The combination of this hope with the professionalization of philosophy in the nineteenth century had a peculiar outcome. Whereas earlier scholars had valued Xenophon as a non-philosophical source for Socrates, scholars in the last two centuries have become increasingly interested in Socrates and Plato *as* philosophers, with the result that Plato's writings alone have seemed worth consulting for evidence about his teacher as philosopher. The Socrates of Plato's dialogues has thus become the only Socrates for most people and even for many scholars.

The other consequence is rather paradoxical in light of the first. Even as Plato's dialogues have come to overshadow all other evidence about Socrates, the lingering effect of source-criticism has been to cast their portrayal of Socrates into doubt. And this effect has been shaped by political preoccupations. Knowing, on some level, that Plato's is only one portrait of Socrates, embedded in the texture and purposes of his own writing, students of the dialogues have become suspicious about the accuracy of Plato's portrayal and about his motives in drawing it. Did Plato betray Socrates in putting his own views – contradicting those of his actual teacher – into his character Socrates' mouth? And if so, did he mean to betray him? These questions troubled those writers who were concerned with the relation between Socrates and democracy. But they also opened up a new approach to defending Socrates. For if Plato was the bad guy, the evil prophet of metaphysics or totalitarianism, perhaps a pure Socrates could be preserved as the good guy whose beliefs or commitment or faith could still inspire. As will be shown further in Chapter 4, the democratic celebration of Socrates has often gone hand in hand with the democratic vilification of Plato.

We turn now to the civic questions about Socrates outlined above, which may be roughly summarised thus: was Athens right or wrong to sentence Socrates to death – and was Socrates right or wrong to accept his sentence? Answers can be ranged roughly along a spectrum of those who condemned Athens while exonerating Socrates, those who managed to find something to admire in both, and those who exonerated Athens while condemning Socrates. Of course, just what Athens was, and who Socrates was, and how far they are prototypes for contemporary politics, will be raised in and by every modern answer. The moderns, as we have seen, divide between those concerned primarily with democracy and those concerned primarily with culture and history. And the former followed in the footsteps of the ancients, for whom the question of Socrates' relation to democratic Athens was inescapable.

Athenian politics and the role of Plato: ancient democratic readings

The democratic dimension to the civic question of Socrates and Athens is not a modern invention, the product of some over-eager historian or sociologist. Ancient authors raised it explicitly. Socrates was tried only a few years after Athens had surrendered to Sparta after almost thirty years of war. The Spartans had encouraged a brutal oligarchic coup which overturned the democracy, although the democrats regrouped and recaptured the city a few months later. An amnesty passed by the restored democracy forbade any legal charges to be laid on grounds of collaboration with the oligarchs. But several indictments were brought on seemingly specious charges, designed to circumvent the amnesty and punish acts of anti-democratic treason. That of Socrates appears to have been one of these.

Some fifty years after Socrates' trial, the orator Aeschines declared in passing: 'Gentlemen of Athens, you executed Socrates the sophist because he was clearly responsible for the education of Critias, one of the Thirty anti-democratic leaders ....'[2] Critias, widely regarded as the head of the Thirty who led the coup, had been one of Socrates' intimates, as had been Charmides, another leading associate of the Thirty; and the charge of 'corrupting the youth' must also have evoked memories of the earlier treasonable exploits of his most glamorous follower, Alcibiades. Socrates would seem to have been condemned for the treason of his friends. The implication was that it was his teaching which had led them astray.

In depicting Socrates as an anti-democrat, or at least the friend and philosophical mentor of one, Aeschines – himself a good democrat – casually condemned him. Plutarch reports a similar condemnation by the conservative Roman moralist Cato the Censor some hundred and fifty years later: Cato called Socrates 'a mighty prattler, who attempted, as best he could, to be his country's tyrant, by abolishing its customs, and by enticing fellow citizens into opinions contrary to the laws'.[3] Among the ancients, beginning with Socrates' own contemporaries and judges, this must have been a widespread view. If so, it explains why Plato and Xenophon (among other Socratic writers) had tried so hard to mount a rebuttal in their own writings. Both sought to show that the way Socrates engaged with others was beneficial to the city and even specifically to its democratic political regime.

Xenophon quoted Socrates' response to a Sophist's challenge as to how he could make politicians of others while avoiding political involvement himself: ' "How now, Antiphon?", he [Socrates] retorted, "should I play a more important part in politics, by engaging in it alone or by taking pains to turn out as many competent politicians as possible?" ' (*Memorabilia* I.6.15). Similarly, in Plato's *Gorgias* (521d), as Matthew Arnold would celebrate, Socrates calls himself the only true politician. And in a more subtle vein, in Plato's *Apology* Socrates declares that he has been a necessary 'gadfly' to the 'great and noble' but 'sluggish' horse of Athens, performing a necessary function by his provocative questioning (*Apology* 30e). He goes so far as to propose that his 'punishment' should in fact consist of free meals, like those given to the Olympic victors. Thus the city would recognize his own peculiar contribution to civic welfare. For both Plato and Xenophon, in short, Socrates' way of living had been a boon to his native city, and Athens' murderous ingratitude had been an unconscionable mistake.

Socrates was right, Athens wrong: modern democratic readings

Intolerant Athenians: Enlightenment debates

The fact that Plato and Xenophon had had to fend off opponents who held that Socrates' conviction had been politically warranted was with the fall of democratic power soon forgotten. Most writers from imperial Rome until (and into) the eighteenth century assumed that the death sentence had done Socrates an injustice. The legend reported in the *Life of Socrates* by Diogenes Laertius, that the Athenians had immediately repented of their deed, banished or executed his accusers, and erected a bronze statue in his memory, was grist to this mill.[4] In the eighteenth century, a handful of historical scholars began to question whether the Athenians might at least have had good reason for killing Socrates.[5] But more typical was the attitude of the great Enlightenment scourge of the clerisy, François Arouet de Voltaire. Voltaire in some moods darkly suspected Socrates of having been a charlatan. Nevertheless he was among those who, condemning what Athens had done in killing Socrates, found the explanation resonant with parallels for his own day. For Voltaire, it was the religious prejudices of the Athenians that led them to condemn the free-thinking rational philosopher Socrates, just as the Catholic Church had censored Galileo. That the

Athenians were pagans detracted nothing from the comparison for Voltaire; if anything, it made the behaviour of the purportedly enlightened Christians worse. In *Socrate* (1759), a tragedy in three acts first published pseudonymously, he dramatized Socrates as a martyr to religious fanaticism.

Opposition to this sentimental cult of Socrates as the hero of reason, as dear to the German Enlightenment as to the French, soon arose. And its most dramatic manifestation was in a text born of a confrontation in which the Enlightenment world view was challenged from within. In 1758 the young Enlightenment protégé Johann Georg Hamann returned to Königsberg from a visit to England having been converted to a radically anti-rationalist form of Christianity. An old friend and patron visited him to try to persuade him back to the path of reason (as it were, back to both faith in reason and to rational faith), accompanied by the young philosophy teacher Immanuel Kant. Hamann was not to be persuaded. His defiant reply, defending his new radical faith, took the form of a book entitled *Socratic Memorabilia*, in which he reclaimed Socrates for his own views against those of Kant. Hamann proclaimed that 'the ignorance of Socrates was sensation (*Empfindung*)'. Such ignorance did not lead to the gaining of rational knowledge; it was helpless unless graced by the only true completion and satisfaction for ignorance: faith.[6] So Socrates was not the proud rationalist admired by Voltaire. He was rather to be understood, through the words of Saint Paul, as one who knew that he did not know and loved God anyway.

For Voltaire, Socrates stood for free thought against popular religious superstition; for Hamann, he embodied the need for religious faith as against popular religious scepticism. Hamann's was the lonelier voice, as the image of Socrates as free-thinker otherwise dominated the century. In England, John Toland founded a 'Socratic Society' to pursue rational inquiry into ethics and politics, and Socrates became an icon of the *Spectator* founded by Addison and Steele. One or two voices questioned the opposition that Voltaire, if not the English writers, had posited between Socrates and Athens. The young Johann Gottfried Herder, for example, full of enthusiasm for the French Revolution in 1791, insisted that the greatness of

Socrates was due to the existence of democracy, 'for Socrates was no more than a citizen of Athens, and all his wisdom was only the wisdom of an Athenian citizen'.[7] But the more typical impact of the Revolution was a bitter revival of the image of Socrates as a martyr to the mob. Robespierre had passionately admired Athens. Yet as the Terror unfolded, he and other would-be tribunes of the people saw themselves fall victim to the mob, (in their eyes) the ignorant and selfish people, who were distorting the true course of the Revolution. And so Robespierre and others cast themselves as incipient martyrs, following in the footsteps of Socrates, Cato, Phocion and other ancients whose heroic virtue had brought them to their death.

Admirable Athenians, mistaken about Socrates

Typical in this respect of the French Enlightenment (which in this matter was at one with the German), Voltaire was no democrat. His call for religious freedom and an end to tyranny over thought was addressed to Frederick the Great and, less hopefully, to the French kings. And while democratic leanings had been stirred in England among a substantial minority by the American Revolution and the creed of radical dissent, the initial impact of the French Revolution was to extinguish them under a blanket of fearful repression. Devouring its children, the Revolution struck fear into the political class across the Channel. But such fear also helped eventually to engender reform of the franchise at Westminster. And although such concessions were initially couched rather as defences against democracy than as contributions to it, the Reform Acts brought many thinkers gradually to accept democracy as a legitimate, inevitable political form and language.

As the political climate slowly warmed toward democracy, a radical Member of Parliament worked to thaw the intellectual climate too. George Grote's pathbreaking, cosmopolitan *History of Greece* (1846-56) challenged the conventional portrait of Athens (which had been shrilly renewed in English histories of Greece published in the wake of the French Revolution) as a society of mob rule. In so doing he set the stage for the re-evaluation of Socrates' relation to Athens, his own account of which was subtle and complex. Grote managed to find grounds for admiration of both Athens and Socrates, although, as we shall see, he did so to some extent by sacrificing his admiration of Plato.

Athenian democrats had long been condemned as fickle in their allegiances, emotional and volatile in their decisions. Grote argued that the democrats had been cool and reflective judges, changing their minds only when new evidence or arguments gave them good reason to do so. Again, ancient democracy had long been condemned as a cover for class rule by the poor. Grote defended the poor sailors of the fleet as the backbone of the democracy and, moreover, as having forced the rich to accept the 'constitutional morality' which was the condition of free government in England, the United States and the Swiss cantons in his own day. Appealing to the characteristic English pride in the jury system, he urged that the Athenian juries had been run on the same principles. Theirs was not a form of mob rule, but rather a system of constitutional self-government of which modern liberals could and should approve.

Despite inevitable cavils, Grote's history was a stupendous popular and critical success both in England and abroad. The main lines of his defence of Athenian democracy were made available for later proponents of democracy to use, and as we shall see in Chapter 4, the twentieth century brought forth a number of works attacking Plato as an enemy of just the sort of healthy democracy that Grote had celebrated. Grote himself, however, refrained from converting his defence of Athens into an automatic attack on Plato and Socrates. Far from it: his next major work was a critical but admiring evaluation of *Plato and the Other Companions of Sokrates* (1865; Grote revived the practice of transliterating Greek 'kappa' with English 'k').

In the Preface to this three-volume work, Grote defines philosophers as 'individual reasoners' who 'dissent from the unreasoning belief which reigns authoritative in the social atmosphere around them'.[8] Though the Athenians were politically capable, they were, like any other society, entangled in a tissue of conventional prejudices reinforced by the drastic sanctions of public opinion.

24

2. Who Was Socrates?

The community hate, despise, or deride, any individual member who proclaims his dissent from their social creed, or even openly calls it in question ... The orthodox public do not recognise in any individual citizen a right to scrutinise their creed, and to reject it if not approved by his own rational judgment. They expect that he will embrace it in the natural course of things, by the mere force of authority and contagion – as they have adopted it themselves ....[9]

And who was the dissenter *par excellence*? Socrates. His death was due to the sheer suspicious stupidity which infects every community. Grote was willing to endorse some of the blame which Voltaire had pinned on religion. He saw this not as a matter of manipulative priests, however, but of residual religious prejudice corrupting the otherwise sound instincts of the jurors. Society, not democracy, was to blame. Democracy as such was friendly to scientific free thought and conscientious dissent. But all democracies had to learn to resist their own worst instincts. To borrow an expression from Grote's friend John Stuart Mill in his defence of liberty written in the same decade, it was the tyranny of the majority which killed Socrates.

Mill himself, in the course of that defence of liberty, bracketed Socrates with Christ as comparable victims of judicial iniquity: in Socrates' case, the man who had deserved the best of his age, the master of all subsequent philosophers, had been put to death as a common criminal. Mill's mention of Socrates' impact on philosophy deserves explanation. Mill's remarkable education, conducted by his father James, included study of Platonic dialogues in Greek from the age of seven. And both James Mill and his son, together with Grote, found in the dialogues a Socratic method of logical argument and criticism which they valued and adopted as their own.[10] As Grote observed, the dialogues were marred by doctrinal assertions of political and theological views, but their living spirit lay in the spirit of scepticism which they breathed. Invoking the character of Socrates, Plato had opened the path to intellectual freedom. This invocation of the Socratic method is alive today in American law schools, on the Internet, and indeed everywhere critical thinking claims to be taught. Its identification, as a method for clear thinking and social criticism, against the tradition of mystical Neoplatonism which we shall meet further in Chapter 3, was an achievement of the group of 'philosophic radicals' to which Grote and the Mills belonged. They recovered and valued the sceptical side of Socrates while yet being fair to Athens.

Athenian (and Victorian) Philistines

John Stuart Mill's contemporary, Matthew Arnold, cast the relation between Socrates and his society in similar, though somewhat bleaker and more defiant, terms. Arnold was classically liberal in his politics but elitist in his view of culture. He saw Socrates as standing for the higher intellectual culture of self-reflection. This was conceived not as the precise logical method celebrated by Mill and Grote but as a general paean to the powers of self-awareness, a standing rebuke to the complacent materialism Arnold loathed. And could not Arnold himself and a little band of followers be the Socrates(es) of their own day? Might that not be a higher vocation than the degrading pursuit of political power?

> Socrates has drunk his hemlock and is dead; but in his own breast does not every man carry about with him a possible Socrates, in that power of a disinterested play of consciousness upon his stock notions and habits, of which this wise and admirable man gave all through his lifetime the great example, and which was the secret of his incomparable influence? And he who leads men to call forth and exercise in themselves this power, and who busily calls it forth and exercises it in himself, is at the present moment, perhaps, as Socrates was in his time, more in concert with the vital working of men's minds, and more effectually significant, than any House of Commons orator, or practical operator in politics.[11]

Though it is roughly the same argument, how different is the defiant and isolated tone here from that of the practical, civic-minded Grote and Mill, both of them House of Commons orators in their day. Arnold used Socrates to model a determinedly un-political politics, one which could temper and refine the banal excesses of democracy. The consolidation of a nineteenth-century concern with 'culture' provided Arnold with a new dimension in which to defend philosophy as useful. Philosophy could help the city (in practice, when Arnold wrote, the gradually but inexorably democratizing British state) by edifying the souls of its members. Socrates had been the most useful of citizens, and the modern metropolitan Athens still had need of him.

'It is Socrates, not Plato, whom we need'

Grote had defended both Athens and Socrates. Arnold had been more hostile to the philistine majority in Athens, as in British democracy, seeing both as a standing threat to his icon of Socrates. Both admired Plato, but Grote bitterly rebuked Plato's failure to find a place for free speech in the ideal city depicted in the *Republic*. In so doing, Grote laid down the lines of a classic position: that Plato in the *Republic* committed the 'great betrayal' of Socrates.

> In the Platonic Apology, we find Sokrates confessing his own ignorance ... But the Republic presents him in a new character. He is no longer a dissenter amidst a community of fixed, inherited, convictions. He is himself in the throne of King Nomos: the infallible authority, temporal as well as spiritual, from whom all public sentiment emanates, and by whom orthodoxy is determined ... He now expects every individual to fall into the place, and contract the opinions, described by authority; including among those opinions deliberate ethical and political fictions, such as that about the gold and silver earth-born men. Free-thinking minds, who take views of their own, become inconvenient and dangerous. Neither the Sokrates of the Platonic Apology, nor his negative Dialectic, could be allowed to exist in the Platonic Republic.[12]

Many writers in the last two centuries have adopted this uncompromising stance, the great majority of them Anglophone. It is salutary however to find, adopting a similar position, the Weimar lawyer

Max Alsberg, who described the accusers of Socrates in terms of the influential psychology of the crowd put forward by Gustave le Bon. Alsberg celebrated Socrates as the first accused to be sacrificed to an error of justice. He regretted only that Socrates had not chosen to make clear the existence of a higher law than the unjust law written on a 'scrap of paper'.[13] A more famous German speaker adopting this 'Socrates-as-good-democrat versus Plato-as-anti-democrat' approach was the Austrian Karl Popper, who wrote in English for an Allied readership during the Second World War. Popper famously declared his credo thus: 'It is hard ... to conceive of a greater contrast than that between the Socratic and the Platonic ideal of a philosopher. It is the contrast between two worlds – the world of a modest, rational individualist and that of a totalitarian demi-god.'[14] Popper's influential and controversial attack on Plato will be considered further in Chapter 4. Here we consider a more typical descendant of Grote (and one on whom Popper explicitly drew), a man who would become yet another Westminster M.P., Richard Crossman.

Whereas Grote and Mill had been independent of Oxbridge, Crossman was an Oxford don, who became a liberal Christian socialist and served as a prominent Labour M.P. after the Second World War. His book *Plato Today* (1937) will be considered further in Chapter 4. Suffice it to say here that he saw Plato as a dangerous partisan of what would inevitably become 'a polite form of fascism'. Plato was the real enemy of democracy. Socrates, who had been ordered to die by the democracy, was the victim of a tragic misunderstanding. He himself was democracy's friend – a critical friend, undoubtedly, but then criticism was the life-blood of democracy. For Crossman, Socrates was an independent-minded liberal, committed to free inquiry and social progress, who was betrayed by Plato, the systematic would-be architect of an illiberal regime.

Crossman cleared away any ambiguity in Arnold's judgment of Socrates as a democrat. For both, he was the icon of the individual who challenges the thoughtless prejudices (cultural or political) of his society: the decent man who has no truck with political cant or cultural philistinism. 'Socrates showed that philosophy is nothing else than conscientious objection to prejudiced unreason.'[15] Crossman also used the age-old comparison between Socrates and Jesus to new purpose. Whereas for many previous thinkers, Socrates in his imperfection could only herald the perfect Christ, Crossman treated the two figures as parallel. Both were dissident, dogged individuals, who wrote nothing but were written about and in the process betrayed by their great disciples, Plato and Paul. In the end, one cannot serve two masters. Maintaining loyalty to Socrates and to Jesus will free their followers from the cramped castles of their disciples' dogmas. As Crossman's book on Plato concluded, 'It is Socrates, not Plato, whom we need.'[16] For Crossman, nothing in Socrates' life or philosophy was fundamentally opposed to Athens. The Athenians had tragically misunderstood necessary (if harsh) criticism as deadly opposition.

Socrates and Vietnam: right to dissent, wrong to obey

Crossman and Grote thought Socrates symbolized a critically supportive relation to democratic politics and culture: in short, that he was the model Enlightenment citizen. With Socrates thus enthroned as the image of the ideal philosopher, in the late twentieth century the war in Vietnam made the need for such a model acute. A generation of American writers, seeking to evaluate or legitimate their stances on the war, were attracted to Socrates as the model of a philosopher who had loved justice and acted justly.

In Plato's *Crito* (49a-e), Socrates declares his loyalty to the principle that it is better to suffer injustice than to commit it. This moral standard appealed to the protesters against the war in Vietnam. It seemed to give them moral justification for opposing the commands of the federal government, in particular for resisting the draft and the punishments for draft-dodgers, and perhaps for protesting against the injustice of the war by breaking other laws. Moreover, in Plato's *Apology* (29d), Socrates proclaims that were the jury to order him to cease philosophizing, he would disobey them rather than disobey the command of the god to remain at his appointed post. Here was a brave hero, a resister of injustice, to put alongside his spiritual god-children Thoreau and Gandhi as patron saints of civil disobedience.

Yet other aspects of the *Crito* threatened to throw a spanner in the works of this promising case. The context for Socrates' enunciation of the principle concerning doing and suffering injustice is his rejection of the proposal made by his old friend Crito that Socrates should be sprung from prison and taken safely into exile (an occurrence not uncommon in ancient Greece for those with wealthy and influential friends). And when the arguments which Socrates puts forward in his own name, hinging on the principle mentioned above, fail to convince Crito, Socrates makes a long speech in the name of the Laws of Athens. The personified Laws claim that all citizens brought up in their jurisdiction owe them obedience as their true parents and masters (51b-c) and that Socrates had, by remaining in the city on reaching the age of maturity, made an agreement to obey them. How, the anti-Vietnam generation asked themselves, could the champion of justice have articulated such reactionary arguments?

One common strategy was to try to show that the conclusions were only apparently reactionary, or that the argument would in other circumstances yield the right radical results. David Hume had pointed the way with his observation that Socrates 'had built a *tory* consequence of passive obedience, on a *whig* foundation of the original contract' (i.e., when imagining what the Laws of Athens would say to him about escaping from prison, Socrates postulates that he had made an agreement with the Laws that he must now obey).[17] That whig foundation had now to be shown capable of supporting different conclusions. Within this strategy, the principal tactic was to argue that the *Apology* did support genuine civil disobedience, in that disobeying an order to stop philosophizing would have been a public and meaningful act for Socrates. Despite appearances, such an act would not have been selfish: in continuing to philosophize Socrates would continue to benefit the city. And this stance was not contradicted by the *Crito*, where Socrates refuses to engage in an act of escape which would not (involving, as it would, lying and secrecy) have been proper civil disobedience at all.[18]

The *Apology*, then, was declared the fundamental Socratic document, which showed that Socrates saw that some moral obligations had sometimes to be overridden in the name of an even more urgent and higher demand of justice. With these and other arguments, many contributors to the debate managed to persuade themselves that Socrates could be rightly enrolled in the ranks of those who had resisted British authority in the American Revolution and who were then pursuing peaceful civil disobedience in the streets outside. But the thoughtful voice of Gregory Vlastos demurred.

Vlastos, a liberal Christian and a classical scholar, had satisfied himself that the *Crito*'s apparent defence of utter obedience was compatible with resistance to grave injustice. And he maintained Socrates as his philosophical hero to his dying day. Yet in his old age, he told a Berkeley graduating class that the students of the 1960s had taught him that Socrates' commitment to resist injustice had not gone far enough. He urged the Berkeley students 'to accept what Socrates never did: the concurrent, not easily harmonized, claims on us of the intellectual's lonely search for truth and the corporate struggle for justice'.[19] Socrates had resisted injustice only when the doing of it threatened to dirty his own hands. The lesson of the civil rights and anti-Vietnam movements was that, as a model for fighting social injustice, neither the tactics nor the ethics of Socrates went far enough.

Despite Vlastos' troubled reflections on his hero, admiration for Socrates dominated the late twentieth-century American debate. Such admiration tended to treat him as a straightforward democrat, glossing over the tensions in his civic life of which the ancients had been so viscerally aware. One voice, however, that of the crusading journalist I.F. Stone, joined admiration for Socrates as a freethinker to a reluctant insistence that he had indeed promoted anti-democratic attitudes, and that the democratic Athenians had been right in perceiving this. In his book *The Trial of Socrates* (1988), written after learning Greek in his eighth decade, Stone held that Athens was nonetheless wrong to have killed him: not because Socrates was not an anti-democrat (he was), but because in so doing the city was untrue to its own proud civic tradition of free speech. Stone's defence of Athens against simplistic celebration of Socrates was in the tradition of Grote's defence of Athens against simplistic condemnation of democracy. Both managed to appreciate both sides of an ancient conflict, while concluding nonetheless that Athens had been wrong in what she did.

Seeing both sides (or just blaming Socrates): the cultural and historical readings

Grote and Stone were unusual in their ability to respect both Socrates and Athens. Most of the portraits of Socrates considered so far portray him as Athens' wrongful victim. In each case the picture of Athens presented is subtly different. Athens could be seen – and implicitly compared to modern states – as pagan clerisy (Voltaire), as vulnerable to popular prejudice (Grote), or as susceptible to self-righteous political cant (Crossman). But all agreed that Athens was wrong in putting Socrates to death, whatever her reasons for doing so. Even as ardent democrats, Grote, Mill, Crossman and Stone were sure of that. And such accounts typically implied a direct parallel between the relation of Socrates to Athens and the relation of intellectuals and philosophers to the regimes of their own day. Socrates had played a valuable civic part, and Athens had been wrong to suppress him at the end; so too the contemporary critic (in all of these cases, arguably, a thinly disguised version of the writer himself) was right and valuable in his strictures against his own society.

But the nineteenth century also saw the rise of a new and more complicated approach to Socrates and Athens. This, which we see at its apogee in Hegel and Nietzsche, treated Athens not as a stand-in for contemporary states but as a particular ancient historical culture, which had been destroyed by the more 'modern' figure of Socrates. Socrates was indeed the bearer of political and philosophical Enlightenment, but this brought in its train the destruction of older Greek values. On these views, then, Socrates was guilty of having corrupted ancient Athenian culture, and the Athenians' attempt to defend themselves against this was understandable and valid, even if their defence was doomed in the long run.

These approaches can be described as 'topical'.[20] They portray Socrates as a turning point in world history, a *topos* (Greek for 'site', in this case a rhetorical site) on which the meanings of our culture hinge. Socrates as the first rationalist, as the first to connect ethics and reason, as the first to challenge the happy naivety of his fellow Greeks: these kinds of stories show us a far more complicated set of motives for Socrates' life, and by extension for his death. Like Grote and Stone, Hegel saw merit in both sides, while others reversed the blame altogether, making Socrates the guilty perpetrator of cultural subversion instead of the innocent accused.

A tragedy of its time: Hegel

Hegel's lectures on the history of philosophy exemplify the topical approach: the aim is to put Socrates in his historical place, understanding his significance in terms of his advance on his own time. For Hegel, Socrates' life and death are equally important. Alive, he inaugurated a new phase in the evolution of the world spirit, introducing subjective self-consciousness to the evolving comprehension of what is rational and universal. Dying, he clashed with the principle of the state, which was not yet prepared to cope with a conscious individual challenge to its ethical life. The conflict between Athens and Socrates was marked by a tragic necessity. Tragic, in Hegel's understanding, because both had right on their side: Athens the right of its naive folk-religion and family piety, Socrates the right of rational progress from objective ethics to subjective morality.[21] Necessary, because Socrates teetered on the brink between the old and new orders. He was a herald of the coming subjectivity which would bud in Christianity and flower, for Hegel, in Luther's Reformation. But he was still a child of Athens, and the ethos which had formed him was ripe but not yet ready to die.

The aim of Socratic conversation, according to Hegel, was to help his interlocutors uncover their own rational self-consciousness. Reason's goal was to think of the universal (which the pre-Socratics had acknowledged) as the good (the moral viewpoint which was peculiar to Socrates). Socrates had not worked out the full substance of his own view. But even to posit it was to undermine the naivety and so the strength of Greek ethics.

The Greeks were not corrupt priests, nor a wild mob, nor philistine barbarians. In a variation on the view of J.J. Winckelmann,

33

whose passionate admiration of Greek art was noted in Chapter 1, Hegel saw the Greeks as beautiful children living unselfconsciously in the sunlit public world of their own perfection. No one before Socrates had challenged the integrity of their world. Even Antigone, who died for disobeying her ruler's decree, had only opposed one Greek principle (civic supremacy) in the name of another (familial piety). She did not set herself up as an individual who could use her reason as a final tribunal of moral principles. But this was what Socrates heralded. His call for a rational morality subverted the self-evidence of Greek values without as yet having anything positive to put in their place. No wonder the conflict was tragic. Greece could not but lose, yet Socrates (speaking for Reason) was not yet in a position to win. Both were right according to their own lights.

Hegel went so far as to justify not merely the verdict alone, but even the charges which were in fact laid against Socrates in the trial. He read the charge of 'corrupting the youth' not, as others had and later would again, as a specific reference to homosexual love. Instead, for Hegel, who had read his Aristophanes, this charge referred to Socratic education, which alienated young men from their fathers and so weakened the respect and filial piety crucial to Greek mores. The other charge, that of not worshipping the city's gods and introducing new ones, Hegel also justified by reference to Socrates' *daimonion*. Hegel saw this as the incipient voice of universal conscience. Yet Socrates himself did not yet understand it, and attributed to his *daimonion* what he should have attributed to his own moral self-awareness. The *daimonion* was something unconscious, which Socrates externalized, but which the Athenians rightly saw as competing with their own revered oracle at Delphi (despite Socrates' reference to the Delphic oracle in the *Apology*, 20e). As such it competed with the established gods and so was legitimately condemned by the city.

The clash was inevitable. And only someone with a short-sighted sense of history would imagine that, in ordering Socrates' death, Athens had won. In the long run, she and the rest of Greece lost, ruined and corrupted, by the spirit of subjectivity which Socrates had unleashed. Yet reconciliation would ultimately arrive. It would come in the mind of the spectator, in this case the later spectator who reads about Socrates' execution and is brought to acknowledge the right on both sides.[22] Hegel suggests that the clash between Socrates and Athens is really resolved only in modernity, when thanks to Lutheran religion and Prussian politics, the best of Greece – the political, cultural, and aesthetic harmony between city and individual – could be reconciled with subjectivity in the ideal modern state. As citizens of that state we can appreciate both sides of the old Greek conflict. By comprehending Socrates' fate we place ourselves, topically, beyond him. He can be admired, but on this historicist picture he is no longer needed. He belonged to a particular moment in antiquity and with that his work was done.

Optimist or pessimist? Nietzsche

For Nietzsche, like Hegel, the confrontation between Socrates and Athens was a confrontation between rationalism and antique Attic culture. And even less than Hegel was Nietzsche concerned with the democratic aspect of Athens. He was captivated by the values and world-view of antique society, what he called the 'tragic view of life', which had persisted into the height of the democratic age. But Nietzsche despised Hegel's determinism and understood the nature of Socratic rationalism rather differently. Most of all, whereas Hegel was certain that his own philosophical position at the pinnacle of history placed him far beyond the earnest efforts of Socrates to awaken the Idea, Nietzsche saw Socrates as someone who had succeeded in the same kind of gigantic effort that he himself had embarked upon: the transvaluation of values.[23]

Socrates had given the Greeks an equation between reason, virtue and happiness, to replace their crumbling inchoate beliefs. Nietzsche longed to give, or at least to herald, a new constellation of values which could make the world meaningful again in the face of the crumbling Christian churches which had inherited and then undermined the Socratic equation. In fact it was Plato who had introduced transcendentalism to the Forms and so, for Nietzsche, to the Church, as will be shown in Chapter 3. But the fundamental, earthshattering shift from tragic acceptance of the world's irrationality, to the ambition of universal happiness through reason, was to be charged to Socrates. Nietzsche therefore could not leave Socrates alone, could not simply put him in his place; at one stage the modern writer noted that he was almost always fighting a battle with Socrates.

As a brilliant young philologist at the University of Basel, enchanted with Richard Wagner's music-drama, Nietzsche posed the problem of Socrates in terms of culture. Greek culture, Nietzsche proposed in his first work, *The Birth of Tragedy out of the Spirit of Music* (1872) embraced more than the sunlit Winckelmannian picture of classical poise. This was one element, the 'Apollonian', but it floated on the waves of 'Dionysian' orgiastic passions. Greek tragedy harnessed both elements to console the spectator and encourage him to go on living. Tragedy invigorated; it did not justify. But Socrates (working with the playwright Euripides, who undermined tragedy from within) proclaimed a new standard for art: to be beautiful, art must be reasonable, justified by reason rather than motivated by instinct.

Before Socrates, the Greeks instinctively knew the limits of reason and expressed this awareness in their myth and dramatic poetry. But Socrates undermined this tragic world view. He asserted that reason could and should rule in the soul, subordinating passion altogether, and that reason, not tradition or authority, could determine ethical judgements. Reason alone could tell one how to live, a prescription that was inherently universal in the sense that it claimed authority over everyone. In this way Socrates was the ancestor of the Enlightenment, the 'theoretical man' par excellence. Ironically, reason was not pure in Socrates himself: he was subject to the instinctive prompting of his *daimonion*, though he had made rational consciousness into his creative principle and confined instinct to a wholly negative role. Yet the claim that reason could prescribe a universal morality had in Nietzsche's view been alien to the Greeks, and marked a watershed in the history of ethics.

This picture of Socrates is not unlike Hegel's in the way it pits Socrates as individual against the culture of his society:

Socrates believed that he was obliged to correct existence ...
he, the individual, the forerunner of a completely different

culture, art, and morality, steps with a look of disrespect and superiority into a world where we would count ourselves supremely happy if we could even touch the hem of its cloak in awe.[24]

And Nietzsche also concurs with Hegel that in doing this Socrates had played a crucial role. His contribution was necessary in the sense of being needed at the time, although it was not necessary in the Hegelian sense of being determined: Nietzsche captured the contingent but drastic effect of Socrates by describing it as a stone thrown into the machine of Greek culture. That culture was, alas, already disintegrating, and without Socrates the Greeks would have fallen into 'practical pessimism', a sick loathing of life which would have led to waves of suicide rather than to the further building of culture. Socrates was in fact 'the nub and turning-point of so-called world history' because of his own greatness, not because of historical determinism.[25]

Although he was doing them a service, the Athenians understandably did not recognize this. Yet they were not to be blamed for his death. Nietzsche suggested that the Athenians had wished only to banish him. It was Socrates himself who had sought his own death in order to become a martyr to the cause of reason, thereby incriminating the hapless Athenians in the eyes of posterity (here Nietzsche could draw on Xenophon, who averred that Socrates wanted to die). 'The *dying Socrates* became the new, hitherto unknown ideal of noble Greek youth; more than any of them, it was the typical Hellenic youth, Plato, who threw himself down before this image with all the passionate devotion of his enthusiastic soul.'[26]

Nietzsche returned to the charge that Socrates engineered his own death in one of his last works. *The Twilight of the Idols* (1889) includes a major section on 'The Problem of Socrates', the most extensive discussion outside *The Birth of Tragedy*. Here, however, Nietzsche subtly changed the story. Socrates did not die to pose a heroic example to others, he died knowing that his own mission had failed.

Socrates wanted to die – it was not Athens, it was he who handed himself the poison cup, who compelled Athens to hand him the poison cup ... 'Socrates is no physician,' he said softly to himself: 'death alone is a physician here ... Socrates himself has only been a long time sick ...'.[27]

The charge of suicide has taken a sinister turn. Socrates is no longer the optimist attacked in *The Birth of Tragedy*; at the end of his life he realizes himself to be a pessimist, who sees life itself as a disease. Nietzsche finds the hint for this reading in Socrates' last words in Plato's *Phaedo* (118a), when, having drunk the hemlock, he asks his friend Crito to sacrifice a rooster to Asclepius, the god of healing, as successfully cured patients traditionally did. On Nietzsche's view, Socrates finally discovered that the rationality he had tried to impart to his city had been useless, in fact harmful. The self-styled physician of Greek culture became in his final hours the patient, grateful for a cure from the only real physician: death. The mission of his life had been misconceived from the start.

To think of Socrates' death as suicide was not without precedent. It found some natural support in the fact that he was commanded to drink poison – a command which he himself had actively to carry out – rather than executed by an outside force. French Salon painters in the last years of the *ancien régime* had delighted in portraying Socrates' death as suicide, along with the suicides of the Roman philosopher-statesmen Cato and Seneca – all admirable acts of philosophers who 'died by their own hand rather than truckle to dictators'.[28] But Nietzsche's diagnosis of suicide was the opposite of the Salon's. The painters depicted it as an act of bravery and public virtue, whereas Nietzsche suggests that it was an act of impotence and private disgust. Why did Nietzsche become keen to impute such mean and pathetic motives to Socrates?

The answer cannot be simple scorn. Nietzsche's involvement with Socrates was far too intimate, obsessive and complicated for that. Indeed at some points in his writing he was more admiring of Socrates than the comments we have just been considering would lead one to expect. In works such as *Human, All Too Human* (1878) and its appendix, *The Wanderer and His Shadow* (1880), written just a few years after *The Birth of Tragedy*, Nietzsche treated Socrates as an exemplar of the admirable type of free-spirited philosophical inquirer rather than as the specific nemesis of a specific ancient culture. There, unlike priests and idealists who arrogantly neglect the needs of the individual, Socrates is shown to have concerned himself with the human, and is held up as a future replacement for Christ, as 'a guide to morals and reason' which would be 'directed towards joy in living and in one's own self'. And in a passage of *The Gay Science*, Nietzsche describes a thought similar to that of *Twilight of the Idols*, but in a kinder and more generous way. Marvelling at the fact that Socrates may have turned pessimist in his last breath, he exclaims ruefully to his reader that 'we must overcome even the Greeks!'[29]

At other points, however, Nietzsche seems to have feared that if Socrates were too admirable, too moderate, too perfectly cheerful, then his own philosophical mission would be undermined. Socrates manifested a faultless unity of character which has exerted an unending fascination for others. While Nietzsche attacked the specific philosophical tenets of that character, he seems at once to have admired and resented Socrates' success in his own project of self-creation, which he, Nietzsche, sought at once to repeat and to surpass. Perhaps the vicious tone of the suggestion in *Twilight of the Idols* that Socrates was really a weak pessimist was a last desperate move by Nietzsche to put Socrates in his place: to put him down and so keep him out of the place of 'cheerful brave philosopher facing death with equanimity' which was to be found somewhere near the mountain hermitage of Zarathustra.

The Athenians as moral heroes: Sorel

In 1889, the year Nietzsche went mad, the iconoclastic French engineer and philosopher Georges Sorel published his first book: a study of the trial of Socrates. Like Hegel and Nietzsche, Sorel held that Socrates had sounded the death knell for traditional Greek ethics. But unlike Hegel, unlike even Nietzsche, Sorel saw no redeeming features in this corruption. Neither Hegel's full-blown historicism, nor even a Nietzschean admission that the Greeks might have been already weakened was to be allowed. Sorel (relying heavily on the work of another French scholar, Alfred Fouillée) dramatized the conflict between Socrates and Athens as one not to be relegated to the historical past. Socrates and Athens stood for opposed moral choices which were exactly those open to Sorel's own contemporaries. So Socrates was not, for Sorel, to be relegated to the historicist *topos* of a past moment in world history, as for Hegel, nor even to be put in his place, as for Nietzsche. He could be identified with a current and recurrent challenge to the society of manly virtue for which Sorel longed. Since not Socrates, but Athens, was to be the model for present-day politics, Sorel exonerated Athens from having killed the Socrates who posed her a mortal threat.

The particular content of this discussion testifies to the moral themes that would remain constant throughout Sorel's dramatic political journey from liberalism, to a kind of radical anarchistic socialism known as anarcho-syndicalism, to fascism (just before the First World War) and then back again to syndicalist-socialism and enthusiasm for Lenin. Roughly speaking, for the engineer Sorel, reason was good so long as it was confined to mechanical improvements. But reason should have nothing to do with morality, which is the domain of heroic virtue fed by myth. Calculating the use of force in a legalistic manner belongs to the bourgeois-capitalist parliamentarian conventions which stifle true morality. Such conventions must be overturned by a pure eruption of proletarian vision and violence.

This stance led Sorel to find Socrates at fault, and to make the Athenians the heroes rather than the villains of the piece. Like Hegel and Nietzsche, he idealized the pre-Socratic Greeks. But he did so on his own terms. He saw them not as naive and beautiful Hegelian children but as morally upright citizen-soldiers, heroes of the legendary battle of Marathon in which the Athenians and Plataeans were victorious over the mighty Persians. These were the admirable men whom the accusers of Socrates wished to restore to moral and civic prominence, and to their honourable ranks belonged also that comic mocker of Socrates, Aristophanes.[30] These men scented the effeminate dialectical subtleties to which Socrates wanted (in Sorel's pungent terms) to reduce their heroic morality.

Correspondingly, Sorel argued that Socrates was not the victim of the Athenian priests as the eighteenth-century free-thinkers had claimed. Rather, Socrates himself aspired to a kind of theocratic power. (Whereas Grote believed that Socrates was a free-thinker, betrayed by the politically ambitious and intolerant *Republic* of Plato, Sorel saw Socrates himself as a would-be autocrat.) According to Sorel, Socrates' own ideal state would have been an 'ecclesiastical' one designed to impose his beliefs on others, as Calvin had done in his Genevan theocracy or the Jesuits in their missions in Paraguay. Not heroes but intellectual quasi-priests would reign, if Socrates had his way, and the result would be moral degeneration and political weakness.

Unlike Hegel, Sorel defended Socrates against the legal charges brought against him. Perhaps his own impatience with parliamentary procedures made him reluctant to admit that the legal trial itself was what mattered, as opposed to its broader moral significance. In any case he offered a defence: Socrates was no atheist, he was orthodox in his religious observance if not in his beliefs, and he did not corrupt the youth into homosexuality (abhorrent to Sorel, who wanted to clear the Greeks generally as well as Socrates from the charge of homosexual love). Still, the trumped-up legal charges emerged from a moral and social context which made Socrates odious to the *demos* (in Greek, the 'people'). His ascetic life, his pretensions to prophetic inspiration, and the general cultural affinity between his activity and that of the sophists, amply justified the people in judging him a symbol of the new ways.[31] For Sorel, Socrates represented the calculating rationalist whom he saw still alive in the trade unionists and parliamentary deputies around him. Such a man threatened to destroy his own culture, and emulating him would bring ruin to that of Third Republic France.

Democracy as individuality: the civic comprehension of the cultural and political

Care for the self

So far we have schematically opposed the democratic reading of Socrates, which made him an icon for contemporary society, to the cultural-historical reading, which in its pure form relegated him to a stage in the development of the past. Sorel's picture of Socrates, however, clearly undermined this opposition, by using a cultural-historical analysis to make Socrates into an icon for his own political position. And indeed, as we saw, Nietzsche sometimes could not resist taking Socrates as a model for his own cultural role, even though at other points he insisted on reading Socrates as a Greek in his own context. The idea that these approaches are opposed is too simple. Historical readings can (and very often have) served implicitly as models for contemporary political action. Similarly, as we shall now see, democratic readings can be developed beyond a simple assessment of whether someone (Socrates) was 'for' or 'against' democracy. By incorporating cultural complexities of the kind sketched by the historical readings, democratic positions can be enriched in their self-understandings and in their under-standings of Socrates alike.

Matthew Arnold's appeal to Socrates as having done more for politics, in the course of his philosophizing, than any M.P., regis-tered an insight of this kind. Opposing the philistine Victorians, Arnold argued that a liberal culture, not a political majoritarianism, was the true soul of democratic politics. Great political benefit could therefore be gained, paradoxically, from a principled anti-political stance. One can discern a similar if simpler manoeuvre in the views of some of the anti-Vietnam protesters. In holding that Socrates in the *Apology* posed a legitimate challenge to democratic majoritari-anism (never mind that the majority was constituted as a jury instead of an Assembly in the actions in question), A.D. Woozley suggested that a higher duty (by implication a democratic one) could sometimes require the breaking of existing law. Such a view would be further developed in John Rawls' *A Theory of Justice* (1971), a work written during the height of the Vietnam War, in which Rawls defends civil disobedience as a democratic act, when laws which should enshrine equality and freedom instead violate these condi-tions of democracy. Such insistence that true democrats might have to oppose democratically-made (unjust) decisions harks back to the kind of complex democratic service that Arnold found in Socrates.

We have seen that Plato's writings had to be separated and distorted to make out a case for Socrates as the first civil disobedient, not least because he did not disobey the sentence of death. The civically minded philosopher and refugee from Nazism, Hannah Arendt, was sceptical on exactly these grounds of the standard American invocations of Socrates and Thoreau as models for civil disobedience. Neither, on her view, was motivated by sufficiently civic motives: Socrates owed it *'to himself'* to stay and die, and Thoreau was similarly motivated by 'individual conscience' rather than 'a *citizen's* moral relation to the law'. Yet while she would reject Socrates as an icon of democratic disobedience, Arendt had installed him in *On Revolution* (1963), her great meditation on the American Revolution, as having modelled a new kind of relation of the individual to himself or herself. Confronting the ever-present possibility of the hidden crime in politics – that is, the possibility that someone might commit a crime but never be known or held to account for having done so – Socrates tried to dissuade his contemporaries from finding this possibility appealing. He did so by inventing a new form of self-awareness, a new way of experiencing and interpreting the self.

> The Socratic solution consisted in the extraordinary discovery that the agent and the onlooker, the one who does and the one to whom the deed must appear in order to become real … were contained in the selfsame person. The identity of this person, in contrast to the identity of the modern individual, was formed not by oneness but by a constant hither-and-thither of two-in-one; and this movement found its highest form and purest actuality in the dialogue of thought … [T]he Socratic agent, because he was capable of thought, carried within himself a witness from whom he could not escape; wherever he went and whatever he did, he had his audience, which, like any other audience, would automatically constitute itself into a court of justice, that is, into that tribunal which later ages have called conscience.[32]

In contrasting Socrates' dialogical self-awareness with that of 'the modern individual', Arendt did not mean to claim that her contemporaries could have no access to such Socratic awareness. Her point was that modernity had caused this capacity to atrophy, as the tendency to evacuate the public realm led individuals to forget their civic (Socratic) identity as well as their civic duties. Feminist writers such as Seyla Benhabib have followed Arendt in invoking the capacity for imaginative self-awareness, and by extension for imaginative awareness of the other, as central to the constitution of properly civil citizens.[33] On this view, which is a kind of psychological extension of J.S. Mill's, democracy which makes no home for individuality is not democracy but majority tyranny.

From 1970 onwards the very concept of an 'individual' or 'subject' was coming under scrutiny in France, not least in the radical historical studies by Michel Foucault of such topics as madness, punishment and sexuality. Foucault developed Nietzsche's idea of a genealogical method which could expose the contingencies of historical change. He described these contingencies as emanating from the exercise of power and discipline beyond the control of any individual subject. Many critics read this as ruling out any individual responsibility or agency, especially when Foucault insisted that the 'subject' itself was constituted by these flows of power. But it has been well argued that the apparent determinism of Foucault's view dissolves when interpreted in light of the inspiration to activism which he and others found in his work; the historical analysis of the effects of power can suggest possible strategies for resistance, which is in any case inseparable from power.[34]

In his last years, Foucault found in Socrates a model for the practice of 'caring for the self' (*souci de soi* in French, from the Greek *epimeleia heautou*, in Plato's *Apology* 29e), which he thought represented just such a possible strategy. Modern individuals might not be morally self-legislating as Kant had hoped, nor wholly altruistic as in Christian or Marxist fantasies. But they could care for themselves and thereby do something small but useful to care for others. The benefit for the city which Foucault discerned in Socrates was not a directly political one, as in Xenophon's account of his training up young politicians. Rather, 'in teaching people to occupy themselves with themselves, he teaches them to occupy themselves with the city'.[35]

Foucault held that this modest and practical activity had been obscured and misrepresented by its association with the famous inscription at the oracle of Delphi commanding 'Know thyself'. For the ancient Greeks, Foucault suggested, this had meant simply 'Do not suppose yourself to be a god', and for Socrates was always related to the practical activity of self-care. For Foucault, Socrates combined the image of a Stoic sage with that of an ancient Sceptic (and both ancient sects themselves had made him their model). As the Stoics believed of the perfect sage, his reason made him supremely virtuous. But in agreement with the Sceptics, he eschewed theoretical speculation. His was a genuinely practical wisdom which enabled him to be virtuous without being a metaphysician or a pedant. It was Plato who later inflated 'knowing thyself' into a dangerously one-sided intellectual concept. To this extent Foucault endorsed the view of Plato as the origin of a fundamental Western mistake, as having betrayed the fundamental values of Socrates, though he held that not all subsequent thinkers had followed Plato in this error and that it was possible for him and his contemporaries to avoid the error as well.[36]

Even greater than his esteem for Socrates himself was Foucault's admiration for the Roman-period Stoics and later Christians who followed in his footsteps, turning to 'care for the self' as a way to survive conditions of political arbitrariness and oppression. And a kindred cry arose at almost the same time from a contemporary world of political oppression, from behind the Iron Curtain shielding Prague. Cut off from the West, the Czechs were struggling to remind themselves that their country had been at the heart of European culture for centuries. In a private course of seminars published in 1979, the great Czech philosopher Jan Patoçka appealed to 'care for the soul' as the crucial tenet defining Europe. Socrates had proclaimed care for the soul as a task on the one hand entirely interior, on the other hand essential for the health of the city.

Patoçka offered a markedly gloomier picture of Socrates' Athens and her prospects than most of the commentators we have considered so far in this chapter: 'The Athenian democracy in his epoch was in reality pierced by the venom of a tyrannical viewpoint.'[37] Socrates had to resuscitate the old Athenian religious and political values by articulating the civic task in a new way. This involved restoring the citizen's sense of conscience and responsibility, which had been dented by loss of political agency. Agency begins with the self and depends upon a metaphysical horizon within which the self resides. Socrates could inspire the Czechs to do the same, to keep their spirits up and cultivate their souls during the long dark night of tyranny.

Socrates' irony, Socrates' death

Patoçka's appeal to Socrates as a hero who resisted civic decline (and suffered political oppression) by cultivating individuality, neatly combines the three major themes of this chapter so far: that Socrates figures simultaneously as the centrepiece of an ethical, a civic, and a cultural story. But although it concluded a section devoted to synthesis and complication, it may seem to be in one sense all too obvious, casting Socrates as the noble hero who deserves imitation and veneration. One cannot but recall at this point a feature of the Platonic Socrates which has so far gone unmentioned: his irony.

As Alexander Nehamas has documented, several of Plato's characters (but none of Xenophon's) accuse Socrates of being ironic. Thrasymachus in the *Republic* objects that Socrates is being ironic in claiming that he and Polemarchus, doing their best to discover justice, deserve to be pitied rather than scorned (*Republic* 337a1-2). Alcibiades in the *Symposium* says that Socrates had ironically rejected his sexual advances and spends his whole life 'ironizing and playing with people' (*Symposium* 216e4). And Socrates himself in Plato's *Apology* says that if he were to tell the court that he could not stop philosophizing without disobeying the god's command, they would think he was speaking ironically (*Apology* 38a1). Nehamas points out that these are not cases where Socrates means simply to deceive, using his irony as a cover for what he really means. Rather his ironic posture is experienced by others as a kind of superiority, one which offers him a degree of freedom.[38] Socrates (often? always?) does not say what he really means, and though his interlocutors suspect and resent this, they are unable to penetrate his true meaning.

46

2. Who Was Socrates?

Nehamas' reading steers between two extremes: the one, that of Hegel, who had suggested that the meaning of Socratic irony was transparent to the reader though not to the other characters in the dialogues; the other, that of Hegel's contemporary and *bête noire* Friedrich Schlegel, who recommended Socratic irony to his fellow Romantics as the only literary attitude that could afford them total freedom.[39] For Hegel, Socrates' irony was purely instrumental; for Nehamas, it was an aspect of his character which remained opaque even to Plato; for Schlegel, the essence of Socrates was his irony.

This last paradoxical view was radicalized even further by the tormented Danish theologian Søren Kierkegaard. In his 1841 Copenhagen dissertation *The Concept of Irony, with Continual Reference to the Figure of Socrates*, Kierkegaard was still under the sway of Hegel, but seeds of his later hostility to the German speculative thinker are already apparent in the originality of his discussion of irony. Kierkegaard sums up his position thus: Socrates' 'irony was not the instrument he used in the service of the idea [as Hegel had claimed]; irony was his position – more he did not have'.[40] For Kierkegaard, as for the scourge of the Enlightenment, Hamann, half a century before, Socrates' position had been and could only have been one of pure negativity. Socrates was ironic through and through. He had destroyed Greek ethics without providing anything to replace it. Thus he had not anticipated Christ – who uniquely would bring something new and positive (the 'good news') into the world – but had only served to clear the obstacles from the latter's path.

For Kierkegaard, then, Socrates' irony signalled that he had occupied a distinct historical niche, that of the pagan who highlighted the need for Christ without yet being able to herald His coming. And his execution was only the ultimate expression of his irony. It was not due to Athenian blindness or venality, but to his own philosophical commitments; it was not a contingent external blow of fate but rather the only way Socrates could make his death consistent with the unremitting negativity of his life. By accepting death as his sentence (indeed, as Nietzsche would argue, by even orchestrating the jury to vote for execution), Socrates accepted a

47

punishment which was utterly meaningless to him and so no real punishment at all. Believing that she had punished him and suffering the opprobrium of future ages for having done so, Athens was the ultimate victim of Socrates' irony.

Such a view of Socrates' death, however, has not been popular. Most have oscillated between the view that death was no real punishment for him because of his cheerful courage and the timeliness of death in old age (Xenophon), and the late Nietzschean view of his death as evidence of his final pessimism and realization of his own failure. A challenge to Nietzsche's reading was put forward by Michel Foucault. Nietzsche had argued that the cock for Asclepius was a sign that Socrates at the last recognized that he was sick of life; his purported rational cure was only a symptom of his own illness. Foucault had to contest this insinuation in order to defend Socrates as an example of the healthy care for self.

Noting that Socrates said that 'we' (not 'I') owed a cock to Asclepius in return for having recovered from illness, Foucault's solution was to suggest that the recovery in question was that of all Socrates' disciples from false beliefs.[41] On this account, Socrates' last words indicated not his sickness but his health: his commitment to the self-fashioning which he had carried out in the company of friends. He was not grateful for death, but he approached it concerned only with his own self-project, the freeing of himself and his intimates from false belief – the project to which he had dedicated his life.

Now it is evident that, as Alexander Nehamas has observed, Foucault's reading downplays the deep vein in the *Phaedo* which compares the body to a prison and death to a release from this prison for the immortal soul. But whether or not Foucault's reading is defensible, it is instructive to see that he proposes a Socrates who remains focused on his own individual self, his self-project, even up to the moment of his death. Not for him to sacrifice himself for his city as a martyr, nor to seek to triumph over it; this Socrates is not a civic hero or victim except insofar as the communal project of self-care which he initiates with friends can be said to have an indirect civic significance. Foucault did not spell out that civic significance in his comments on Socrates' death, though remarks made elsewhere indicate that he saw comparable modern forms of self-fashioning (such as the gay sado-masochism community) as having the ability to resist and deflect the exercise of disciplining power in the name of what might be called freedom. Arendt and Patočka, as we have seen, tied the cultivation of individuality more closely to its civic benefits and role. But they too insisted that it must in the first instance be pursued for its own sake.

Pursuing the possibility of synthesis between political and cultural, the two sides of the civic, with the demands of individuality, reveals that the civic Socrates, the Socrates who criticized and was condemned by Athens, is not one that we moderns can forget. Indeed, it is impossible to prevent readers from making an icon out of Socrates as modern democrats have done. They have done so from the moment of his death, as Julia Annas reminds us, speaking of the thousand years of antiquity in which Socrates was read: 'right from the first Socrates was seen as an adaptable figure, serving as an ideal of the philosopher ... the historical Socrates right from the first greatly underdetermined all the different Socrateses of philosophy.'[42]

What can be criticized, however, are the occasions when ideological tunnel vision freezes Socrates as an icon for a single purpose, severing him from the rich complexities of his history and later understandings of it. Arendt, Patočka and Foucault remind us that the drive to set up Socrates as a pure icon of democracy should not be used to hide the very real questions about what democracy means for individuals and requires of them, or about what democracy needs from philosophy and yet may fear in it. They remind us, in other words, that the civic Socrates should not be segregated from the Socrates of the ethical and religious traditions, that Socrates' public significance grew out of his relationship with himself. It is precisely this paradox which means that Socrates exceeds all our categories. He did not exhaust himself as a do-gooder, yet he did good; he devoted himself to private conversation and self-improvement, yet he became the educator of all Athens; he did not involve himself actively in politics, yet his trial was a pivotal point in the evolution of Athenian civic culture. Ralph Waldo Emerson, at the time of the

American Civil War, a politicized epoch if ever there was one, imagined Socrates as saying:

> I have no system. I cannot be answerable for you. You will be what you must. If there is love between us, inconceivably delicious and profitable will our intercourse be; if not, your time is lost and you will only annoy me. I shall seem to you stupid, and the reputation I have, false … All my good is magnetic, and I educate, not by lessons, but by going about my business.'[43]

The question of how Socrates educates finally returns us to the other theme in this chapter: the relationship between Socrates and Plato. The temptation to freeze Socrates as a pure icon is all the greater because he did not write. Because he expressed himself solely through conversation, Socrates can attract the fantasy of revelation, of an unmediated origin, which we met in Chapter 1. In light of the comments on historical criticism in this chapter, this desire for a pure origin can now be appreciated as, paradoxically, the reverse side of the modern desire for historical certainty through criticism. Socrates' was an oral teaching uncorrupted by the vagaries of written transmission. Anything unacceptable in what we have received of him, therefore, can (must) be ascribed to the wicked or thoughtless actions of his scribes. It is this fantasy of the oral Socrates, the writing Plato, which Jacques Derrida inverted in his *The Post Card*, in which he rings changes on a postcard purportedly portraying Plato dictating to a writing Socrates.[44]

But the inescapable fact that Socrates was Plato's teacher, as he was the teacher of Alcibiades, Critias and Charmides, mocks the modern desire to make Socrates a pure and isolated model of the good against the perverted evil of his followers. For teaching is an impure medium. What the teacher offers mingles with what the student brings, and what the teacher may not recognize as the fruits of his instruction may yet have been stimulated in the student by listening to him. To install Socrates and Plato as the first great teacher-student pair in the history of philosophy is to be unable ever cleanly to distinguish between them. And this in turn is to be forcibly reminded that philosophy lives in interaction rather than isolation, in the development and cross-fertilization of ideas, rather than the hopeless quest to segregate a pure original source. An impure (knowledge of) Socrates is what we have, and the yearning for any other kind is a delusion.

3

Plato on Forms and Foundations: The First Metaphysician?

All things are for the sake of the good, and it is the cause of everything beautiful.

> Ralph Waldo Emerson, 'Plato; or,
> The Philosopher' (1850)

All philosophical idealism is an illness ....
> Friedrich Nietzsche, *The Gay Science* (1882)

The *beauty* in the *Phaedrus*; this side was not touched upon in the myth of the Cave.
> Simone Weil, *The Notebooks* (1956)

Introduction

When Alfred North Whitehead described the history of Western philosophy as a series of 'footnotes to Plato', he meant this as a compliment. Plato was to be credited with laying down the fundamental lines of thought that philosophers have followed ever since. But others, most famously Friedrich Nietzsche, had already turned this evaluation around. Plato had indeed laid down fundamental lines of thought, but his choice of lines deserved no positive credit. According to Nietzsche, Platonism established two fundamental errors as integral to the subsequent philosophical and (Christian) religious history of the West. First, the claim that ultimate reality transcends the world known to the senses: the claim of transcendence. And secondly, the claim that morality is based on this transcendental reality: the claim of foundationalism, that is, that ethics must be founded on the reality described by metaphysics.

53

Instructed by Nietzsche, his followers have attacked both claims as invalid, and have reiterated Plato's guilt for introducing them. The result may astonish any layperson who assumes that Plato remains our model of what philosophy should be. For many writers in the late nineteenth and twentieth centuries, Plato has been the villain rather than the hero of the history of philosophy, guilty of bamboozling almost all subsequent philosophers (except the Nietzschean writers themselves) into believing in his false picture of reality.

The Nietzschean attacks hinge on the notion of the 'Forms' or 'Ideas' (several different Greek words can be translated in either way), and in particular on the way this notion is treated in Plato's *Republic*. Neither in the *Republic* nor in any of Plato's dialogues are the Forms ever fully defined or a 'Theory of Forms' laid out; they are introduced in the main through allusion and analogy. However, they are characterized as eternal, intelligible and explanatory. The beauty of a statue is explained by its relation to the Form of Beauty. To contemplate the Forms is to achieve understanding of what is essential in the architecture of the cosmos. Pre-eminent among the Forms in the *Republic* are the ethical Forms, such as Justice, and above them, illuminating the intelligible world as the sun illuminates the sensible world, is the Good. With the analogy of the Sun goes the analogy of the Line, which contrasts Forms and mathematical objects with the objects of the senses. Together, these analogies have been held to establish the two claims identified above.

Republic VII offers the third and final analogy for the Forms: the famous and haunting image of the Cave. Here, people going about their ordinary lives, achieving what they take to be knowledge through the use of their senses, are compared to prisoners in a cave, who see only the reflections of objects made by a fire. Only by leaving the Cave can such a prisoner free himself or herself from the double illusion (the firelight is not real light, the reflections of objects are not real objects) and come into the light of the Sun (by analogy, the Good) in light of which true reality can be grasped. The political implications of the Cave story – in particular, the suggestion that an escaped prisoner should return to the Cave to rule over those who remain – are addressed in Chapter 4. Our purpose here is to observe that the *Republic* – in particular, the Cave story, the accounts of the Forms, and the discussion of the Good – is the primary locus for the Nietzschean and post-Nietzschean attack on Platonism.

That attack can be summed up in the charge labelled by Nietzsche, in the epigraph to this chapter, as the doctrine of 'idealism'. Idealism, the creed of modern philosophers as diverse as Berkeley, Kant, Schelling and Hegel, asserts that there is a difference between appearances and reality: reality lies somehow beyond, or at least is identifiably other than, all that appears to the senses. The crucial point for present purposes is that idealists have read both transcendence and foundationalism in at least two different ways, one dominant over the other in discussions of recent years. But only the dominant form of each claim has been ascribed to the idealists by the Nietzscheans, dominant forms which the Nietzscheans themselves have established as standard and so fashioned into straitjackets for idealism.

Consider first the case of transcendence. Nietzscheans interpret this as 'dualistic': as positing two worlds separated by an abyss. In this picture, the sensible world is envisaged as a misleading snare of illusion, which should be dismissed as illusory by reference to the other world of transcendental reality. Indeed, basing themselves on the authority of Aristotle, who said that it was Plato who first 'separated' the Forms (from material objects), the Nietzscheans have simply identified the claim of transcendence with its dualistic interpretation.[1] But as this chapter will show, some idealists, drawing on Plato, have themselves explicitly rejected dualism. Instead, they interpret transcendence as 'immanent': the ideas inhere in the material world which they explain and illuminate, being separable from it in thought but not in substance.

For every attack on idealism as dualistic, in the name of the concrete reality of the existing world, another idealist has come along to explain that idealism is itself really the best way to grasp the nature and value immanent in the concrete. (Indeed, idealists themselves have sometimes been quickest to attack dualism, though some do so by emphasizing the way transcendental reality is manifest in the sensible rather than denying its transcendence altogether: a kind of halfway house to immanence.) And as we shall see, support for an immanent reading of Platonic transcendence has been found most often in Plato's passionate account of beauty. Beauty is where the immanence of the transcendent is most tremblingly to be felt, and many Platonizing lovers of beauty have resisted the thought that what they really love is some dualist shadow behind the particular sheen or shape – 'the curve of a rose-leaf', as Walter Pater once put it. On an immanentist view, what beauty has to teach or reveal is inseparable from the beautiful object or person itself. The most recent champion of the immanence of beauty, Elaine Scarry, quotes the Platonically inspired Simone Weil thus: 'He who has gone farther, to the very beauty of the world itself, does not love them [the beautiful things of and in the world] any less but much more deeply than before.'[2]

The case of foundationalism – the claim that ethics is founded on metaphysics – is slightly different. Most Platonists have indeed subscribed to this view. But the Nietzscheans have linked it to a further claim: that ethical goodness is therefore automatically available to everyone. This 'automatic' view, however, is an optional extra, born not with Plato but with Christianity and then (it will be argued) projected back onto Platonism. Platonizing idealists themselves, as opposed to the Nietzschean portrait of them, have characteristically clung to a different, 'aspirational' view of foundationalism. They hold that whatever the metaphysical basis for ethics may be, it is in itself insufficient to guarantee that humans will live ethical lives. Even knowledge of it, purely intellectual knowledge, cannot guarantee this. What ethics requires is rather that humans aspire to goodness, engaging in the moral effort to model themselves and their actions on the good. As we shall see, in this vision of the aspirational Plato, art, love and imagination all play crucial parts.

One can cling to immanence without invoking aspiration, and vice versa. Both have been voiced perhaps by a minority of Platonists, and not all who hold to one also endorse the other. But neither possibility has been countenanced by the typical Nietzschean attack on Plato, an attack which condemns Plato as dualist and foundationalist without stopping to consider the understandings of these charges advanced by devoted readers of Plato themselves. Long-standing traditions of reading Plato, not only the *Republic* but also the *Phaedrus* and the *Symposium*, question whether he was in fact a dualist, and question too the standard interpretation of his foundationalism.[3] The Forms need not be thought to exist in the caricatured Christian heaven against which complaints of dualism (it will be argued) are really directed. They can be seen as a way of articulating the value which structures the ordinary world and which shines forth in its beauty, and they are best grasped by love and the moral aspiration which arises from it. Drawing on voices unheard in the conversations of recent philosophy, these alternative readings cannot be proved conclusively to be true to what Plato meant. But they can be shown to be rich in possibilities of Platonism which the Nietzscheans have not so far conclusively destroyed.

The attack on Platonism: Nietzsche and his followers

Nietzsche against transcendence and foundationalism

Plato measured the degree of reality by the degree of value and said: The more 'Idea', the more being. He reversed the concept 'reality' and said: 'What you take for real is an error, and the nearer we approach the "Idea", the nearer we approach "truth".'

Nietzsche, *The Will to Power*[4]

As we saw in Chapter 2, Nietzsche saw Socrates as the 'theoretical man' *par excellence*, the one who introduced reason into the Greek consciousness and tied it to the question of how to be happy. But it remained for Plato to inflate the Socratic error into a metaphysics which had enslaved the West virtually until Nietzsche's own day. For all his undoubted philosophical greatness, Plato had installed a profound illusion at the heart of philosophy: the illusion of idealism. In the passage quoted above, Nietzsche identified what he took to be the perversity of Platonic transcendence. To say that truth pertains to the ideal, intelligible world of Forms or 'Ideas' is to devalue the 'real', sensible world. By projecting truth onto the heavenly Forms, Plato made the everyday world into a snare of illusion and deceit.

The few philosophers who would, in the city envisioned by the *Republic*, come to know the Forms, are declared therein and thereby to have achieved access to the real truth. And such transcendent objectivity would in turn underwrite their ethical aims and judgments. It is because of the fact (as Plato avows it) that in grasping the Good, they would be grasping transcendental reality, that they would be justified in ruling. For Nietzsche, moral foundationalism was thus characteristic of Platonism. But foundationalism too was actually an illusion based on an inversion. In fact, according to Nietzsche, ethical motives lead people to endorse certain metaphysical beliefs, a process they dress up for themselves in the foundationalist claim that their beliefs about the world guarantee the validity of their ethics. The specific form this took in Plato was his adoption of the Socratic equation that reason = virtue = happiness, that is, that knowledge attained through reason is sufficient for ethical virtue and at least necessary for happiness.

Both key claims of later Platonism – transcendence and foundationalism, both read in the standard way – are therefore, according to Nietzsche, already to be found in Plato's own writings. But Plato's own appropriation of these illusions remained aristocratic at heart. Although the Forms are posited to be transcendentally 'real', only a few favoured individuals are capable of gaining knowledge of them. These few will then have to construct a diet of false belief for the masses in order to keep the polity in good working order and the souls of the many in decent order. Nietzsche applauded this aristocratic element in Plato, while lamenting its corruption by the teachings of the plebeian Socrates. Indeed, he speculated that Plato's idealism may not have been born of illness and weakness but of a peculiar kind of strength: he may have been converted to idealism in order to control his dangerously powerful sensual urges. His own psychology was not as life-denying as the implications of his philosophy proved to be.

By contrast with the special case of Plato himself, however, Nietzsche's diagnosis was that 'we moderns' are not healthy enough to find idealism useful. This is because centuries of having it forced down our throats by Christianity have virtually destroyed the affirmative instincts which Plato still enjoyed. Christianity, Nietzsche declared, was nothing but 'Platonism for the people'. Christianity democratized Platonism by opening the gates of the so-called real world (the world of ideals) to all believers. It was no longer enough that the Forms should be transcendent and foundational: they had also to be open to universal access.

> I find [Plato] deviated so far from all the instincts of the Hellenes, so morally infected, so much an antecedent Christian – he already has the concept 'good' as the supreme concept – that I should prefer to describe the entire phenomenon 'Plato' by the harsh term 'higher swindle' or, if you prefer, 'idealism', than by any other ... In the great fatality of Christianity, Plato is that ambiguity and fascination called the 'ideal' which made it possible for the nobler natures of antiquity to misunderstand themselves and to step onto the *bridge* that led to the 'Cross' ... And how much there still is of Plato in the concept 'Church', in the structure, system, practice of the Church![5]

As Nietszche described it, the Church carried out the programme of Platonism with a double twist. On the one hand was added a universalist promise, that the truth would be available to all believers; on the other, a caste of priests, who monopolized the right to translate the sacred 'truth' into the vernacular of the many. For as long as it lasted, this sleight of hand gave the masses spiritual consolation and a sense of meaning in life, albeit a meaning which affirmed not the life of this world, but the life of the world to come (dualism at its most extreme). But the will to truth which Plato had unleashed eventually turned against his own ethical postulates. By the eighteenth century, the quest for truth had turned into the growth of science, which then threatened to undermine religion. Science made it difficult for believers to continue to equate reason and virtue. (Consider the problem posed by Darwinism, for example: if evolution was a matter of the survival of the fittest, how could moral behaviour be part of God's plan?) Platonism and its spiritual descendants had steered themselves onto the rocks.

The last-ditch defence of Platonism and Christianity was, according to Nietzsche, the philosophy of Kant. Kant had tried to save the objectivity of moral values and of the knowable world from scientific assault and popular scepticism. His dual strategy was to make morality an autonomous property of the rational will, and to remove reality to the realm of the unknowable 'thing-in-itself'. But in so doing he undermined his own aims. By exposing the otherworldly reality, descendant of the Platonic Form and the Christian God, as useless for human purposes and unable to underwrite ethics, he had opened the door to nihilism. This could be put in our terms as follows: by pushing transcendence to its dualistic extreme, Kant made it incapable of serving any longer as a foundation for morality. As Nietzsche prophesied: 'If Kant ever should begin to exercise any wide influence we shall be aware of it in the form of a gnawing and disintegrating scepticism and relativism ....'[6] It was only a short step from Kant's 'God is unknowable' to Nietzsche's fear that the masses would realize that 'God is dead'. Nietzsche's self-assumed task was to stave off nihilism by saving values from the wreckage of Kantian, basically Christian and Platonist, metaphysics.

To do this required that values be freed from their purported metaphysical foundation, which Nietzsche assumed was the only plank supporting their claim to objectivity. This would undermine the further step, the claim of universal accessibility, which Christianity had instituted: once values were acknowledged as having no base in objective truth, Nietzsche inferred that they could no longer be universally accessible. The 'philosophers of the future' would have to do without the Christian dream of universal sanction, and without the double illusions of Platonism. Instead, the philosopher's task was the creation of and legislation of values for the masses, and the delights of brave and inimitable self-fashioning for himself (as discussed in the case of Nietzsche's follower Foucault in Chapter 2).

Arguably it is this additional claim, the Christian claim that moral values are not only universally valid but also universally accessible, that evoked the greatest part of Nietzsche's ire. Nietzsche claimed to have identified Platonism as the origin of Christianity, but the structure and nature of his hostility point to a projection back from Christianity, of all the features which he detested in it, onto Platonism. In other words, he seems to have fallen prey to the very error he diagnosed in others: that of projecting his own moral animus onto an invented origin which is then held to explain and justify that animus. In fact, Nietzsche sometimes acknowledged that Plato might not have believed in the Forms he posited any more than he (Nietzsche) did, but was rather trying to create and impose values for others. (Compare his struggles with the significance of Socrates discussed in Chapter 2.) But whether Plato believed in his own construction or not, if that construction is freed from the Christian guarantee of universal access, the nature of its commitments to foundations and transcendence must be re-examined.

Heidegger against transcendence

Nietzsche charged Plato with having turned real ordinary being into appearance, and the spurious world of Forms into truth. For present purposes, it can be said that the broad outline of the Nietzschean attack on Platonism as transcendence was continued by Martin Heidegger. If Nietzsche charged Plato with having inverted truth and illusion, Heidegger charged him with having isolated a limited truth – the truth of individual beings – at the expense of awareness of the Being which is their horizon. According to Heidegger, the further twist was that Nietzsche's own positive view was still, unbeknownst to himself, a variation of Platonism: Heidegger, not Nietzsche, was the first to overcome Platonism.

Let us consider the elements of this complex picture. We turn first to Heidegger's analysis of Plato's fateful error and its legacy to later philosophy; next, to his reading of Plato's story of the Cave and of the Good; and finally, return to his diagnosis of Nietzsche as a Platonist despite himself. But before all this, an introductory remark. Heidegger, like Nietzsche, despite diagnosing Plato's work and influence as fatally flawed, did sometimes applaud certain aspects of it. Again like Nietzsche, the aspects Heidegger applauded were those in which he felt Plato showed himself not as introducing something new and dangerous to Greek culture but rather as a typical (or outstanding) exemplar of Greekness. The difficulty for both the German authors was to distinguish Plato as an ancient Greek, historically located in his own time, from the subsequent modern influence of Platonism. Heidegger's lectures on the *Sophist* dialogue[7] in mid-1920s Marburg evince his greatest sympathy with Plato as an ancient Greek. Plato was not uniquely responsible for the baneful establishment of metaphysics; Aristotle deserved some blame too, just as Heidegger's postwar lectures on Parmenides would assign blame to the Romans. Conversely, Plato had, as a Greek, been aware of Being, even though he proceeded to obliterate this awareness in the structure of his theory of truth.

Yet even in his *Sophist* lecture course the outlines of Heidegger's critical approach to Plato are evident, and this brings us to the first major point about Heidegger: his diagnosis of Plato's mistake. Heidegger held that the Greeks had understood truth (*aletheia*) as an uncovering which was simultaneously a concealing. This was a mode which did not reify Being as something eternal and radically opposed to absence; it rather emerged from absence and returned to it. Heidegger's discussion of this notion is often translated as 'presencing'. Heidegger long clung to an etymology in which *a-letheia* was construed to mean 'the absence of concealment', and even after he was forced to admit that this etymology was baseless (the Greek means roughly 'not-forgetting'), a basic understanding of the play of concealing and unconcealing in the presencing of truth continued to pervade his work.[8]

As a Greek, Plato was not unaware of this play of Being as coming in and out of presence. But in Heidegger's view, he had fatally chosen to focus his attention on the *eidos*. This is one of the key terms commonly translated into English as 'Form'. Heidegger pointed out (this time correctly) that in ancient Greek, *eidos* literally meant the look of individual beings, their nature and substance as perpetually present entities. This was the root of Plato's theory of Forms. Attending to the 'looks' of beings, Plato had forgotten the play of presencing and so had contributed to the 'forgetting of Being'. As Heidegger wrote in 'Plato's Doctrine of Truth', appropriating a famous comparison in the *Republic* for his own ends, the disclosure, or unconcealing, of *aletheia* is subjected by Plato to the 'yoke' of the Forms.[9] The result is the invention of metaphysics as the study of the 'being of (individual) beings', which for Plato meant the study of the Forms, though later philosophers would substitute their own favoured entities.[10]

According to Heidegger, Plato held that the Forms were knowable by visual contemplation alone, and imagined that the apparent perpetual presence of the beings made knowledge of them eternally valid. This entrenched a fatefully visual approach to metaphysics. But what metaphysics left out, what its blinkered gaze at the Forms could not capture, was the elusive and temporally shifting horizon of Being itself. By inventing metaphysics, Plato (like Aristotle after him) had accepted only what was eternal as wholly intelligible. Heidegger objected in his first major (unfinished) book, *Being and Time*, whose epigraph is a quotation from Plato's *Sophist*, that only the passage of time made the world and human lives intelligible. The question of the horizon of intelligibility meant that Heidegger was unceasingly fascinated by Plato's parable of the Cave in *Republic* VII.

Heidegger engaged with the story of the Cave and the idea of the Good on many occasions, notably in his essays 'On the Essence of Ground' (1929) and 'Plato's Doctrine of Truth', the latter an article which was based on lectures given in 1931-32 but not published until 1942.[11] His treatment of the two ideas was linked. Unlike Nietzsche, Heidegger accepted Plato's notion of the Good so long as it was read not as a moral value, but as equivalent to the world as such, or as he also says, the ultimate for-the-sake-of. In his 1929 essay, Heidegger averred that Plato had had a glimpse of this in the *Republic*, though he marred this insight by a misleadingly ethical, anthropocentric and utilitarian conception of what 'for-the-sake-of' means. The world is not something that humans contemplate or that directs their action along a certain moral path. It is the horizon and the humble available tool for human action. (In his later writings, after his famous 'turn' to a stance of *Gelassenheit* [calmness, letting-be], Heidegger would emphasize the more passive notion of the 'clearing' in which events and actions can eventuate.) Yet in glimpsing the significance of the world, in the *Republic* Plato had fallen prey to two more fundamental problems.

First, the insight of the Platonic Good, faulty as it was, was wrongly tied by Plato to his even faultier reification of the looks of things, the Forms. As Adriaan Peperzak puts it: 'Plato's pure thought of the good as equivalent to the ultimate for-the-sake-of, which is the world, has been contaminated and concealed by the doctrine of ideas [Forms], which, starting from Plato, has become the core of traditional metaphysics'.[12] And secondly, the Cave wrongly pictures humans as in one of two mutually exclusive positions: either trapped without access to the real, or basking in perfect contemplation of the eternal. In fact, according to Heidegger, once one gives up Platonist delusions of grandeur, one finds that one has been at home in the world all the time. The world is indeed a cave, but only in the sense that it is not unconditioned; it constitutes a horizon for humans. The Cave is not the cave of utter illusion from which Plato dreamed that we might permanently escape to the land of truth. It is partly open, permeable to light and, perhaps, visited by the gods.

Heidegger's most fundamental objection to Platonism, then, was what he took to be its commitment to transcendence. Because, unlike Nietzsche, he did not take ethics to be at the heart of Platonism, he did not attack Platonism as foundationalist. In his attack on transcendence, Heidegger took Nietzsche to have rejected the idea of truth because it didn't correspond to anything 'objective' and 'transcendent' of ordinary reality as Plato had expected. But in this rejection, Nietzsche simply negated the idea of truth as correct correspondence, and so, despite himself, still relied on the essential structure of Platonism. According to Heidegger: 'Nietzsche's concept of truth displays the last glimmer of the most extreme consequence of the change of truth from the unhiddenness of beings to the correctness of the gaze.'[13] In making this judgement, Heidegger signalled that only he himself had managed to escape the mirror-relation of truth and beings in order to hearken to the voice of Being, a voice which in its play of (un)concealing escapes the Platonist discourse of truth altogether.

Pairing Plato with Kant

The influence of Nietzsche's and Heidegger's related indictments of Platonism has been both diffuse and profound. A typical attack on

Platonism, marked by the influence of both great predecessors (though less subtle than either in that it ascribes 'Platonism' wholeheartedly and straightforwardly to Plato himself), is that of Richard Rorty. Alluding to transcendence, Rorty writes in a recent popularization of his views that 'the Platonic quest, the attempt to get behind appearance to the intrinsic nature of reality, is hopeless'.[14] There is no transcendentally dualist world of Forms, no world of Being which the philosopher might be able to perceive beyond the tattered curtains of everyday appearances. Rorty dubs this delusion the idea of philosophy as the 'mirror of nature', the ambition that human intellect could grasp and reflect what is really real out there in the world. (We will see later why this is not an apt metaphor to use for Platonism.)

With Heidegger, Rorty treats the objectivity inherent in Platonic dualism as banefully contemplative: according to 'the Greek (and specifically Platonic) analogy between perceiving and knowing', truth resides in the object rather than being a feature of the way propositions are used in human activity and speech. For Plato, declares Rorty, 'the object which the proposition is about *imposes* the proposition's truth.'[15] And finally, we find in Rorty the anti-foundationalist conclusion that ethics cannot be guaranteed by a Platonist (dualist) metaphysics. The Forms were thought to make morality objective and imperative, Rorty suggests, by imposing it on the humans who succeed in grasping them. But if there are no Forms, then morality must have a different basis. And indeed, morality is not something 'out there'; it is the result of diverse human beliefs and practices, naturally varying with circumstance and so no longer guaranteed to be rationally universal.

So far Rorty's account sums up the accusations of transcendence and foundationalism that we have already met elsewhere. Moreover, like Nietzsche (the case of Heidegger is more complex), Rorty takes Kant to have reinforced and developed further the flawed outlook of Plato. Plato's role as villain is complicated and incomplete. He took the first, decisive step toward idealism. But Descartes made it subjective – the world is knowable only through my beliefs – and Kant marked the final flowering of subjective idealism, destroying its achievements in order to save it. Kant had tried to distinguish himself from Plato, but to post-Nietzscheans such as Rorty, their root error was the same. The war on conventional philosophy which Rorty declares is a war against the philosophical influence of 'Plato and Kant'.

The pairing of Plato and Kant, made by Nietzsche and Heidegger alike, is a significant aspect of the Nietzscheans' attack on Plato but one which has received relatively little attention. Its provenance is a complicated story involving the stance towards Plato and Platonism taken by Kant himself, and its relation to his own philosophical commitments. And it also involves the fact that Nietzsche and Heidegger both served a kind of philosophical apprenticeship at the hands of a teacher (literal or figurative) deeply influenced by both Plato and Kant. Nietzsche admired Arthur Schopenhauer, who had seen that the Kantian world of appearances could be described as the ceaseless manifestation of battling wills (what Nietzsche would later call the will-to-power). But Schopenhauer had not celebrated the ceaseless struggle of the will. Far from it: he had viewed it with horror, recommending escape into contemplation of the archetypal patterns of the Platonic Ideas (frozen will, but frozen into a permanence of form that could inspire the artist). Similarly, Heidegger's great teacher, Edmund Husserl, had recommended attending to the pure phenomena of consciousness (a Kantian theme) in which Platonic patterns could be discerned. Both Nietzsche and Heidegger reacted against the combined Kantianism and Platonism of their teachers. But both did so by postulating a Kant and a Plato who had more in common, and along different lines, than their teachers had claimed.

To understand the link between Kant and Plato from Kant's point of view, the story must begin with the establishment of Neoplatonism in the early centuries CE. At the peak of the Neoplatonist tradition which powerfully influenced the first six centuries CE, Plotinus and Proclus taught their disciples to seek mystical unity with the One, the fountain of the system. The Neoplatonic One remained impassive and perfect while its plenitude overflowed to more imperfect and eventually material spheres. Human tranquillity lay in loving and communing with the divine; human creativity reflected its divine source. The influence of this system, which for more than a millennium shaped the way in which Plato was understood, began to collapse under Enlightenment criticism in the late eighteenth century, though it survived well enough to influence German absolute idealists (Hegel and Schelling), and later the poet W.B. Yeats. Neoplatonism embodied the claims of transcendence and foundationalism, though it was a discipline for initiates rather than a programme for universal access of the kind instituted by Christianity. (Proclus was bitterly anti-Christian, although Neoplatonism served St Augustine as an intellectual path towards the Church.)

To Kant, in the eighteenth century, 'Platonism' was identical with Neoplatonism, and the latter with metaphysical dogmatism of a mystical and enthusiastic kind. 'Platonism' became for Kant 'the proper name of metaphysics',[16] the pure form of the dogmatism which had been locked in a sterile and repetitive battle with scepticism throughout the history of philosophy.[17] Each side simply asserted its beliefs without being able to prove them rationally to the satisfaction of the other. And the most recent dogmatists, such as Leibniz (himself deeply influenced by Plato), had maintained naive versions of both classic Platonist claims. Dogmatists in Kant's day, as he saw them, held to the objectivity of moral values as rooted in the transcendent nature of reality.

Kant believed that his own critical philosophy was a new departure: the first to escape both the Scylla of dogmatism and the Charybdis of scepticism. His 'critique of pure reason' advanced a new account of objective knowledge and a new form of transcendence, purified by the critical approach. The conventional dualist image of the Forms as discrete metaphysical objects, floating in a kind of Christian heaven, was exposed as hopelessly naive by Kant's strictures about the unknowability of things-in-themselves. His 'critique of practical reason' meanwhile mounted a similar onslaught on the conventional picture of foundationalism. Rather than seeing ethical truths as enjoying some kind of free-floating independent existence, Kant grounded their objectivity in the self-legislating powers of reason of the will. Hence Kant judged himself to have escaped the ordinary errors of transcendence (when insufficiently critical) and foundationalism (when insufficiently attentive to the self-grounding quality of ethical norms). In line with his new picture, he identified a new role for the Ideas (named after those of Plato): the Ideas were ideas of reason, including the ideas of free will, God, and the soul, which were rationally permissible to postulate even though they could never be proved empirically. Basing himself, then, on a critique of the nature and limits of human understanding and the power of reason, Kant believed these tenets of his philosophy to be justified, in contrast to those of dogmatism which were merely asserted. So the critical philosophy was not simply an opponent or a negation of Platonism, or of any other dogmatism. It was able to surpass and escape it.

The idea that Platonism had to be reversed or surpassed rather than simply opposed became central to the post-Nietzscheans.[18] But they refused to accept that Kant had for his part succeeded in it. The distinction between appearance and reality survived, even structured, Kant's critique. We as humans have access only to the appearances, the 'phenomena' as both Kant and Plato called them. We have no way of knowing the causes of these phenomena. For Plato these were ultimately the Forms; for Kant, more generally, they were the 'things-in-themselves'. By maintaining this distinction, Kant's philosophy, despite his own best intentions, represented only a more advanced form of Platonism, not a fundamental alternative to it.

Now some idealists, in particular Hegel, had rejected the distinction between appearance and reality, while maintaining idealism in the sense that it is the Idea or Spirit which constitutes ultimate reality.[19] By the late nineteenth century, however, Hegelianism was dead in Germany, while Kantianism had been revived. Nietzsche accordingly attacked the Kantian distinction between appearance and reality, and the doctrine of the thing-in-itself, as still clinging to a transcendental dualism. And he linked this charge to the same charge against Plato, even though the accounts of ultimate reality in each case were very different. By so linking Kant to Plato, Nietzsche was able to introduce the second idealist plank of foundationalism into his attack on Kant, despite the fact that the charge of foundationalism is difficult to square with the structure of Kant's self-legislating ethics. Both Kant and Plato held ethics and metaphysics to be objectively true, but the source of that truth was in neither case, arguably, a dualist one, nor was its structure necessarily foundationalist. The result of this typical paired attack on 'Plato and Kant' is a kind of hybrid, with features which belong to neither philosopher. Both are labelled as dualists and as foundationalists committed to a guarantee of universal moral access, though Plato (as argued below) may not have been a dualist, Kant was not a(n ordinary) foundationalist, and Plato may not have been committed to the guarantee of universal access at all. The modern attacks on Plato and Platonism cannot be understood without seeing them in the context of this heavy-handed assimilation to Kant, an assimilation which confuses our understanding of both.

A final irony is yet to be presented. Nietzsche and company were not the first to find Kant's system wanting. From the moment Kant wrote, other philosophers had been unhappy with his postulation of the 'thing-in-itself', which seemed to contravene everything else Kant had taught about the active powers of the human mind. And in the course of the nineteenth century, philosophers otherwise sympathetic to Kant had identified further weaknesses in his views. In his moral philosophy, which relied on the human will to prescribe a law for itself, Kant sought to escape the Platonic postulation of moral values as external while still maintaining their universality. But in the process he gave up any substantive account of the good. And Kant's unfinished critique of judgement hinted at the role of art and imagination in ways that called (not least to artists) for further development.

And here lies the irony: many nineteenth-century Kantians decided that the best way to repair these defects in Kant was to turn to Plato. They had two choices in so doing: to construe Platonic transcendence along fashionably Kantian lines, imputing to Plato the 'correct' understanding of transcendence which Kant had revealed (the Marburg Neo-Kantians would take this path). Or they could accept Kant's criticism of literal accounts of transcendence while still chafing at the rigid and abstract structure he offered in its place. In this case, to search for a more sophisticated version of transcendence in Plato – one which avoided Kantian criticism while improving on the Kantian alternative – appeared a plausible and attractive aim. In short, Kant thought he had got beyond Platonic dogmatism; his sympathetic critics built themselves 'modern Platos' to mend the modern Kant; and their unsympathetic Nietzschean critics in turn declared a plague on both their houses. This complicated story will unfold in the course of the themes examined in this chapter. We begin with the question of immanence, and then move to the question of the relation between ethics and those immanent Ideas, taking in love, art, beauty and imagination along the way.

Against the Nietzscheans: Platonic Forms as immanent

Against the tyranny of the visible

The challenge to conventional dualism begins by recalling a well-established feature of Plato's thought: his adoration of mathematics, and in particular of the recently discovered glories of Euclidean geometry. Geometry was reputed to have been central to the curriculum of Plato's Academy. And in the dialogues we find appeals to mathematical knowledge as a model of understanding and truth. In the *Meno*, for instance, when Socrates recruits a slave to demonstrate recollection of what the soul knew before birth, he takes a geometrical proof as the object of the experiment. And in the *Republic*'s analogy of the Line, a comparison (admittedly highlighting differences as well as similarities) is drawn between Forms and mathematical objects.

For some nineteenth-century readers of Plato, understanding the Forms on the model of mathematics had the potential to correct over-literal interpretations of transcendence. Perhaps the Forms were not to be construed as objects to be seen out there, penned up in a heavenly realm. Instead, they could be seen as 'a concept of the structure and function' of the cosmos, not of 'substance', being better compared to music or geometry than to painting or sculpture.[20] Already in sixteenth- and seventeenth-century England, Sir Philip Sidney and his great-nephew Algernon had been fascinated by Plato's mathematical interests and imagery. In the same vein, Samuel Taylor Coleridge, who imbibed Plato on his own while at Cambridge and later studied with the leading German Platonizers of his day, held the 'despotism of the eye' to be a major stumbling block to metaphysical understanding, anticipating Heidegger on this point by a century. But rather than ascribing a visual (mis)understanding of the Forms to Plato, he saw Plato as having sought precisely to overturn such naivety. Plato had loved music and 'geometric discipline' and recommended them to his followers precisely in order to attune them to an intelligible reality pervading the sensible world. In his Platonically inspired form of Christianity, Coleridge clung to the notion of transcendence as that of an animating mind or spirit in the cosmos.[21] But his appeal to music and geometry implied that such transcendence should be construed as part of the intelligible dimension of the world rather than as isolated in some heaven far above it.

While Coleridge attacked the 'despotism of the eye', his American disciple Ralph Waldo Emerson refined rather than rejected the visual model of transcendence. Recall the analogy drawn in *Republic* VI between the visibility of material objects in the light of the sun, and the intelligibility of the Forms in the light of the Good. One might naturally speak in the latter case of intelligibility to the 'mind's eye' (indeed this English metaphor derives from Platonism). But it is crucial not to confuse ordinary sight, a function of bodily sense, with this special (in)sight of the mind. Emerson urged exactly this point. He celebrated Plato's conception of 'second sight' – the privileged insight into the intelligible structure of the world. And he averred that such 'second sight' had special links with the study of geometry as a way of uncovering the intellectual structure of the world.[22] Emerson's appeal to geometry, like that of Coleridge, indicates an attempt to divert naive misunderstandings of transcendence into more fruitful insight into the intelligible structure of the universe.

The call of beauty

For Coleridge and Emerson, the disciplines of music and geometry could reveal the intelligible structure of the world to human intelligence. But many of those seeking to reinterpret Platonic transcendence in the nineteenth and twentieth centuries have focused on the way the world itself attracts the human desire to understand: in other words, on the phenomenon that 'beauty is a call'.[23] Diotima's speech, recounted by Socrates in the *Symposium*, proclaims that loving beautiful people and things is the first step on a path which can lead the aspirant eventually to encounter and love the Form of the Beautiful itself.

Setting aside the powerful force of love for the moment, it must be acknowledged that, strictly speaking, the relation between the Form of Beauty and beautiful things is no different from the relation between, say, the Form of Equality and equal things. In each case, the Form must be somehow manifest in, or related to, particular things if it is to explain their characteristics. (Even dualists must acknowledge this, though they would urge that the Forms neverthe- less exist separately in an ideal realm.) But the sheer sensual sway of beauty makes one feel that the Form of Beauty is nothing chill or abstract, and can help us appreciate the way it animates the sensible world. As Elaine Scarry writes in a Platonizing vein, beauty is 'some- thing life-giving, lifesaving', which confers aliveness on the beholder even as the beholder confers a special life on the beautiful object seen.[24]

Appreciation of the beautiful can modify one's understanding of Platonic transcendence. The Forms may exist apart from the sensi- ble world, but they must always be bound up in relation to it. Such sensitivity to the tangible, worldly manifestation of the Forms, and in particular of Beauty, was characteristic of the English Romantic poets who followed Coleridge. Lamenting the untimely death of Keats, Shelley invoked the way in which beauty and love shine through the visible universe:

> That Light whose smile kindles the Universe,
> That Beauty in which all things work and move,
> That Benediction which the eclipsing Curse
> Of birth can quench not, that sustaining Love
> Which through the web of being blindly wove
> By man and beast and earth and air and sea,
> Burns bright or dim, as each are mirrors of
> The fire for which all thirst ...
>
> *Adonais* (1821)[25]

3. Plato on Forms and Foundations

This theme was summed up in 1926 by William Ralph Inge, a leading if iconoclastic Anglican clergyman, Dean of St Paul's and Fellow of King's College Cambridge:

> As soon as the seen and unseen fall apart and lose connection with each other, both are dead. Such a severance at once cuts the nerve which makes the Platonist a poet.[26]

For Dean Inge and the tradition he evoked (his book was entitled *The Platonic Tradition in English Religious Thought*), the visible world is not to be abandoned by leaping across the abyss to the intelligible world. Both should be cherished as they are indissolubly connected by a bridge built of the living tissue of beauty.

The recovery of beauty and its intimations of Platonic immanence were fostered by the mystical vision of Neoplatonism, which shaped the great translation into English of Plato's dialogues by Thomas Taylor in the early eighteenth century – the translation read by Blake, Coleridge and Keats. Although Neoplatonism advised contemplation of the One, that One was connected by a kind of overflowing to each lower level of reality, resulting in an immanentist view of the material world. Yeats, above all, instinctively quickened to the possibility of Neoplatonic immanence. For how, ultimately, can one tell the individual from the Form, the particular from the universal, if all one ever encounters in the flesh is the particular? As Yeats asked in his poem 'Among School Children' (*The Tower*, 1928): 'How can we know the dancer from the dance?'

The image of dancing as an immanent display of Form – a kind of bodily expression of the structure of music – was not new when Yeats used it. His poem was anticipated by the writings of another Irishman, Oscar Wilde. Like Yeats, who earlier in 'Among School Children' remarks on Plato (as distinct from the Neoplatonists) thinking 'nature but a spume that plays/ upon a ghostly paradigm of things', Wilde at times construed Plato as typical of the body-hating dualists they abhorred. In his mock-Platonic dialogue, *The Critic as Artist* (1890), Wilde's character Gilbert attacks the conventional bloodless picture of Platonic transcendence thus:

The world through which the Academic philosopher ... leads us astray ... is not really an ideal world, but simply a world of abstract ideas. When we enter it, we starve among the chill mathematics of thought ... Who, as Mr Pater suggests somewhere, would exchange the curve of a single rose-leaf for that formless intangible Being which Plato rates so high?[27]

Yet having swept this false picture of dualism away, Wilde's Gilbert later identifies himself with Plato's philosophy of art and eros in education. And he reads the body as pervaded by soul, in the way that all life is pervaded by Form. (The problem of the relation between soul and body exhibits many parallels to that between Forms and particulars.) Here is Wilde's character, sounding uncannily like the immanentist voice of Yeats:

It is not merely in art that the body is the soul. In every sphere of life Form is the beginning of things. The rhythmic harmonious gestures of dancing convey, Plato tells us, both rhythm and harmony into the mind.[28]

The 'concrete universal'

Whereas Yeats' immanentist leanings derived from Neoplatonism, Wilde's came from the teaching of Walter Pater at Oxford: the doctrine of a Platonizing aestheticism which pushed one step further the liberal Platonism Pater himself had learned from Benjamin Jowett. Pater and Jowett will both be considered further below, and Jowett again in Chapter 4. Here, our concern is with an immanentist Plato developed by another of Jowett's students and later colleagues, the philosopher Thomas Hill Green, who aspired to establish a new understanding of the Platonic Forms which could move philosophy a step beyond Kant.

Green aspired to an eclectic kind of synthesis: roughly, a Hegelian reading of Kant which could be improved by, and made consonant with, the teachings of Plato. The improvement to Kant would consist in getting rid of the 'great embarrassment' of Kant's philosophy, the thing-in-itself. Kant, as we have seen, had clung to a sharp dualistic distinction between the appearances and the things-in-themselves, the unknowable transcendent entities which were obscurely meant to count as the causes of the appearances (also known as the 'phenomena'). Green contended that the cause of any phenomenal object must lie not in a shadowy transcendent realm but in the object's 'relation to all phenomena, in the system of nature'.[29] But there was still work for the Platonic Ideas to do. The Ideas should be reconceived as 'concrete universals', understood as the ideal dimension manifest in any particular object.

This notion of a 'concrete universal', a universal existing in but not apart from a particular, was deeply influenced by Green's readings of Aristotle and Hegel. It is in effect an attempt to have one's cake and eat it on the question of transcendence, balancing on the boundary between transcendence and immanence. The universal 'really exists', in that it is discernible in a particular (as the structure of a sonata is discernible in hearing it played), but it only ever exists as manifest within a particular and never as a separate entity. This can be described as immanence, though it is an immanence allowing for the views of geometry and music which we saw Coleridge advance: universals are not separable except in thought. However Aristotelian it sounds, Green advanced the idea of 'concrete universals' as the correct if sophisticated way to interpret the Platonic Ideas.

In practice, Green had put the accent on the term 'universal' in the 'concrete universal'. Pater, and in the next generation Wilde, pinned their faith more vehemently to the 'concrete' (curved rose leaf) element in the compound: only concrete individual particulars, and above all those exhibited in art or criticism, could satisfy the sophisticated contemplative. And the precise details of Green's idealism were swept away by the leading light of the next generation of Oxford philosophy. F.H. Bradley moved from Greenian idealism to a kind of absolute rational pantheism. Yet he remained faithful to a Greenian conception of the profound significance of Plato as a corrective to Kant. A friend would say of Bradley that he re-read Kant in light of an immanentist Plato, understanding the thing-in-itself not as remote and otherworldly dualism but rather in light of its 'true Platonic meaning of that which is most fully and determinately experienced'.[30] Bradley himself declared his brand of Platonic immanence thus: 'The Reality itself is nothing at all apart from appearances ... they are its revelation.'[31]

Against the Nietzscheans: Platonic ethics as aspirational

So far we have focused on beauty as it has been used to modify accounts of Platonic transcendence. But in almost all the writers so far considered, following Diotima's speech as reported by Socrates in Plato's *Symposium*, the immanence of beauty has been equally significant in terms of its incitement of love. Consider the link between immanence and love drawn in Pater's *Plato and Platonism* (1893). Pater acknowledged that Plato had been swayed by the transcendental (dualist) tendency in earlier Greek philosophy. But he held Plato's genius to have consisted in his ability to hold the drive toward the One in tandem with the appreciation of the Many. This was the Many of the manifold visible world, which Plato knew through loving it. 'Now Plato is one for whom the visible world thus "really exists" because he is by nature and before all things, from first to last, unalterably a lover.' Loving the visual world, he was drawn up to become a lover of the invisible world of the Forms, but he was a lover still, 'and therefore, literally, a seer, of it, carrying an elaborate cultivation of the bodily senses ... into the world of intellectual abstractions ...'.[32]

Pater still admitted the existence of abstractions, but using an Emersonian comparison between sight of the visible and (intellectual) vision of the intelligible, he insisted that love is the connection between the beauty of youths or art and the abstract world of Forms. A critic true to his own aestheticist creed, Pater was most interested in works of art as the worldly manifestation of beauty. Others, such as Coleridge, had appealed more generally to the creative power of the imagination which generated both art and religion, drawing paradoxically on Platonic recollection as a wellspring for the creative mind. And the twentieth-century philosopher and novelist Iris Murdoch would emphasize the ethical dimension of love of the beautiful as it leads on to love of the Good. We shall consider accounts of Platonic love as a generative force and then these several manifestations of it in turn.

Considered together, these readings of Plato articulate a vision of ethics as aspirational. It was suggested earlier that what Nietzsche and his followers most abhorred was not merely the universality of Platonist-Christian ethics, or even their metaphysical foundations, but the guarantee that everyone will easily be able to adopt them. 'Believe and ye shall be saved.' The aspirational Platonists did not reject the objectivity or even the universality of ethics, and most though not all of them have still held that ethics are rooted in the nature of reality. But by emphasizing the moral effort required to respond to encounters with goodness and beauty by creative action, they avoided giving the kind of easy guarantee to those of feeble moral will to which Nietzsche objected in Christianity. An aspirational picture of Plato sets out the Good as a moral aim, attractive to us as an extension of our love of beauty, and challenges us to live up to it. So aspirational Platos change the focus away from the intellectual quest to identify foundations, to the kind of quest to shape and discipline one's life which is not all that far from the forms of self-fashioning advocated by Nietzsche or his follower Michel Foucault. In what follows we will examine love, art and imagination as paths by which such moral aspiration is expressed and developed.

The power of love: Diotima's speech

As stated earlier, love as a Platonic motif comes above all from the speech of Diotima, a fictional priestess, which Socrates claims to recount in Plato's *Symposium*:

> This is what it is to go aright, or be led by another, into the mystery of Love: one goes always upwards for the sake of this Beauty, starting out from beautiful things and using them like rising stairs: from one body to two and from two to all beautiful bodies, then from beautiful bodies to beautiful customs, and from customs to learning beautiful things, and from these lessons he arrives in the end at this lesson, which is learning

of this very [Form of] Beauty, so that in the end he comes to know just what it is to be beautiful.

Symposium 211e

As we shall see in more detail, Diotima further describes the love of beauty as generative. It leads humans to wish to create – either to procreate or to create works of art or philosophy or deeds of virtue.

It would be difficult to exaggerate the literary influence of Diotima's speech over the centuries. It influenced Augustine's discussion of Christian love, and the visions of Dante and Petrarch which descended from it. Its central place in the Platonic canon was established by the greatest Renaissance translator of Plato (into Latin), the Florentine Marsilio Ficino, whose translations and commentaries taught generations of readers to revere Plato. Ficino's commentary on the *Symposium* was probably his most influential. This account of the power and nobility of love was quickly seized upon by courtiers and poets, especially those in liege to female rulers. In the sixteenth century the circles of Marguerite de Navarre and Catherine de' Medici urged poets to compete to express the divine aspect of their ladies' beauty and the enlightening power of love. While study of Plato had crossed the Channel earlier (and we shall look at its political influence on Thomas More in the next chapter), the first figure in English literature to make the themes of love and beauty (rather than religion, metaphysics, or politics) the keynote of his Platonism was Spenser.[33] The tropes of Platonic love and beauty swept through Elizabethan and Jacobean England. They were vividly revived by a modern courtier, the German poet, friend of Hegel and passionate Hellenist, Hölderlin, who apostrophized his beloved Susette Gontard (the wife of his employer) as Diotima.

Ficino's reading of Diotima's speech, which so deeply influenced all these accounts of Platonic love, was itself still deeply Neoplatonic. But Neoplatonism shrank during the course of the nineteenth century under the impact of sceptical questions and new post-Kantian philosophical programmes, and its last great exponent was probably Yeats. Twentieth-century readers of Diotima have had to puzzle out new lines of interpretation for themselves. We will con-

78

sider two aspects of these recent readings: their views of transcendence, and (on this point in direct descent from Ficino) their positions on whether Diotima reserves her highest praise for what we today call homosexual or heterosexual love.

Diotima on transcendence

Iris Murdoch was educated in an Oxford very different from that of Green, though it is tempting to imagine that the latter's Platonism somehow remained in the ether to nourish her. In the Oxford of the 1950s the symbiosis between Plato and Kant had been sundered, and Kantianism had, as Murdoch saw it, run amok. Kantianism and its spiritual offspring such as existentialism admitted only a bare, rigid, unrealistic picture of the moral life. All that mattered was exercising the will, which created the validity of values simply by choosing them. There was no place for love, for beauty, for an objective Good, for the roles of habit and moral perception. To find homes for these fundamental aspects of human experience, Murdoch reverted to Platonism as the only viable form that Christianity could take in the modern world (a neat reversal of Nietzsche's diagnosis). She considered the ascent of love described by Diotima to be exemplary of the moral growth which the moral life requires.

> 'Falling in love', a violent process which Plato more than once vividly describes (love is abnegation, abjection, slavery) is for many people the most extraordinary and revealing experience of their lives, whereby the centre of significance is suddenly ripped out of the self, and the dreamy ego is shocked into awareness of an entirely separate reality.[34]

Fergus Kerr, who quotes this passage, comments that Murdoch commends falling in love as a first step in the painful process of getting one's ego to appreciate the reality of other people and the moral demands made on us by 'the authoritative [and objective] Good'. Kerr further points out a significant contrast between Murdoch's endorsement of what she calls 'unselfing', and another reading of

Diotima's speech which criticizes its aspiration to the transcendence of individual human particularity.

The latter reading belongs to the contemporary American philosopher Martha Nussbaum. Her influential book *The Fragility of Goodness: Luck and Ethics in Greek Tragedy and Philosophy* (1986) explores the way some ancient Greek writers acknowledged the vulnerability of human virtue to accidents which might befall the particular persons or things or projects one loves, while others tried to deny or resist it. Plato is the example *par excellence* of the latter camp. Discussing the *Symposium*, Nussbaum describes Diotima's aim as the conversion of our erotic desire from particular objects to contemplation of the beautiful, a conversion which would make it invulnerable to mortal change and misfortune. And she contrasts this aim with that found in another speech in the dialogue, given by the then-golden boy of Athens, Alcibiades. Alcibiades describes his love for Socrates, his desire to sleep with him, and his pain when Socrates – his mind on the higher things described by Diotima – rebuffs this desire for erotic interchange with him. Nussbaum eulogizes Alcibiades' awareness of the value of love for the bodily particularity of a unique individual, and points out what would be lost if this love were simply subsumed into love of Beauty as such.

As Kerr brings out, Nussbaum's concern with 'transcendence' in this and later discussions is with the aspiration to 'transcend finite humanity', an aspiration which she takes to deny and destroy the value of human individuality. This is different from the theme of Platonic transcendence as defined at the outset of this chapter, which is concerned with whether the Forms are separate from or immanent in the sensible world. But the two senses of transcendence are related. Postulating a separate world of ideal Forms can, as Nietzsche decried, tend to the disparagement and denial of the value of the sensible world, including the bodily particularity and individuality of potential loved ones. But must a Platonic view of love disparage individuals? Another modern reader of Diotima would deny that Diotima's speech should be read to disparage falling in love with an individual at all. But before turning to this feminist reading advanced by Luce Irigaray, we must consider the tradition of homoerotic interpretation of the *Symposium* against which she reacted.

Homoeroticism in the Symposium

In another passage of her speech, given through the mouth of Socrates, Diotima proclaims:

> Now, some people are pregnant in body, and for this reason turn more to women and pursue love in that way, providing themselves through childbirth with immortality and remembrance and happiness, as they think, for all time to come; while others are pregnant in soul ... and these are pregnant with what is fitting for a soul to bear and bring to birth ... wisdom and the rest of virtue ... moderation and justice.
>
> *Symposium* 209a

We met the question of homosexuality in Chapter 1, noting the state of Colorado's calling of witnesses to testify that Plato had condemned it. A hundred years before, in 1895, Oscar Wilde (whose immanentist Platonism was invoked earlier in this chapter) defended himself against charges of 'gross indecency with another male person' by defending male love as the highest form of love, 'such as Plato made the very basis of his philosophy', in an impassioned speech which won from the courtroom a wave of spontaneous applause and which onlookers believed he had modelled on the apology of Socrates.[35] Wilde's speech has been celebrated as the crystallization of a new form of late Victorian homoeroticism, which turned the liberalism of J.S. Mill and the Hellenicizing liberalism of Benjamin Jowett into the demand for a higher male spiritual love.

The issue of *paiderastia* (the Greek practice of older men becoming the lovers of youths) had long dogged Plato's reputation (and had been attached also to the name and reputation of Socrates). Indeed, Greek culture as a whole was often seen as morally dangerous or dubious for its toleration of this purported vice. What complicates the reading of Plato in particular is that the Athenian practice of pederasty (as it is translated) clearly involved carnal sex, whereas

81

Plato's dialogues seem to recommend sublimation of sexual desire into a spiritualized communion. This discrepancy had long been conveniently overlooked by those who wished to mock Plato, such as the Roman satirist Lucian, or to condemn him as immoral and anti-Christian, such as the Church Father Tertullian. Renaissance courtiers simply transferred the homoerotic passion described by Plato to the love of men for women which Diotima also mentions, though seemingly in a lower rank of value: producing mortal children rather than immortal virtues. And when the leading light of Oxford Platonism, Benjamin Jowett, confronted this difficulty, his moralizing interpretation of Plato drove him to mis-translation and prevarication in his commentaries on the dialogues in question. The *Phaedrus*, he said, which clearly describes love between men and youths, could be regarded as raising the question, 'Is marriage preferable with or without love?'

Such temporizing could not conceal the meaning of the text from the very pupils in whom Jowett was attempting to instil both historical awareness and a liberal sense of individuality. Dowling comments that 'the philosophic or intellectual transcendentalism that the Oxford reformers had located in Plato ... could be extended, as Pater and Symonds both immediately saw, to the ideal education of the Platonic or Socratic doctrine of eros'.[36] John Addington Symonds and Walter Pater, the leaders of this 'Greek movement', had been Jowett's pupils, and his tutorials along with the many debating societies of Oxford in the halcyon years between 1854 and 1877 awakened a passion for spiritual and intellectual intercourse. (Jowett himself, on hearing rumours of a love affair between Pater and a pupil, would punish the latter and sever relations with the former completely.) The 'Greek movement' which manifested itself in Pater's learned works and in fevered undergraduate 'Uranian' poetry, invoked homoerotic passion as a part of the richest education, the broadest culture, the most liberal development of individuality to which Hellenism could contribute.

Dowling's instructive discussion misses one dimension of the Oxford Plato of this time: the fact that, as shown above, the moral transcendentalism of Jowett had already been linked to the metaphysical immanence of Green and, in a more aesthetic vein, of Pater.

Pater's invocation of rich sensuous sensation against abstract theory must be seen as part of a re-reading of Plato as an immanentist as well as a pederast. Indeed, the point is that the two themes were indissolubly linked. The immanence of male beauty constituted the very path along which male souls were led upwards in their moral and spiritual quest. The defence of homosexual love in this case develops an aspirational Plato on the basis of an immanentist one.

It is interesting to compare the Oxford ambience with that of King's College Cambridge, where Oscar Browning and Goldsworthy Lowes Dickinson (whom Dowling mentions only briefly) formed very similar societies of intimate intensity between students and dons. In Lowes Dickinson's unpublished and undated manuscript, 'A [Platonic] Dialogue [on homosexuality]', a middle-aged Cambridge graduate, complaining of his son's homosexual proclivities to his old college friend, discovers that that friend (who has remained a bachelor don) had been in love with him himself for years. The don recalls discovering what 'Greek love' had meant at school: 'I reread the *Phaedrus* and the *Symposium* with my new lights, and found there everything I had found in myself. My love became like a flower expanding in the sun ....' The delicate question of the bodily aspect of such love, never unambiguous in fevered Oxford, is broached outright. At first, the erstwhile lover says, the bodily feelings were there, though the soul longed only for an ideal relationship: 'The body indeed I think was what it should be, the wood of the instrument over which the strings of the soul were stretched.' And he resists the erasure of the sexual element from Plato: 'You may call that [Platonic love], if you like, a love without sexual expression, but you cannot call it a love without sex', going on to insist that Plato's proscription of sexual expression was unjust and impossible for some. When the son, Elliott, enters, it becomes clear that as one of a new generation, he is having sex with his lover, with whom however he manages to maintain the relationship on a higher spiritual plane as well (describing why his lover won't give up the chance to go to India, he says 'and of course one wouldn't sacrifice anything important to this thing. That would be like men and women').[37]

Dickinson's experience at Cambridge seems to have been troubled by the same issues that perplexed the ardent youth of Oxford. On the one hand, they shared the conviction that homoeroticism among men was spiritually superior to love between men and women, a conviction rooted in a reading of Plato; on the other hand, they were fearful of the thought, also deriving from Plato, that sex between men might ruin or threaten the very spiritual achievement that their love had betokened.

Heteroeroticism in the Symposium

If the 'Greek movement' found in Diotima's speech the aspiration to a higher spiritual love between men, the sexual expression of which was problematic, a living French feminist re-reads that speech to find intimations that the truest spirituality would lie in sexual love between man and woman. Luce Irigaray proposes that the wonder which traditional Christianity ascribes to the encounter with God, is actually to be found in the freedom of heterosexual passion, in which two beings discover themselves to be unsubstitutable for one another. Such passion has been deformed by the imposition of male forms of spirituality and economy, but represents the proper path to the only appropriate form of the transcendental. Irigaray names this the 'sensible transcendental' which can explode and evade metaphysical dualism. The post-Nietzschean aspiration to destroy dualism is here married to profoundly Platonic themes; the most evident aspect of the 'sensible transcendental' lies in beauty. 'Beauty itself ... confounds the opposition between immanence and transcendence ... as an always already sensible horizon on the basis of which everything would appear.'[38]

To readers of this book, such a claim should not appear novel or radical; it follows in the very traditions of immanent and beauty-loving Platonism that we have been discussing. Indeed, the notion of a 'sensible transcendental' bears a striking resemblance, in terminology and function, to Green's concept of the 'concrete universal'. Though it must be acknowledged that the aspiration to find such a middle way or third term owes much to Hegel and what he learned from Aristotle, Irigaray like Green is determined to make this notion at home in a Platonic text. The place where she finds it most explicitly is, of course, in Diotima's speech, a speech which she ascribes to the woman Diotima, while observing that Socrates, in reporting it, may have 'distort[ed her words] unwittingly or unknowingly'.

In recognisably post-Nietzschean language, Irigaray claims that Diotima initially succeeds in identifying love as an intermediary, one which will not be swallowed up by dialectic but is always 'already there'. Diotima says that love (eros) is something between mortals and immortals, between poverty and wealth, between ignorance and wisdom, and Irigaray comments that love is precisely what permits movement from one apparent opposite to the next. Love allows immortality to enter mortal life. Diotima's first example of this is sexual love between man and woman. 'The union of a man and a woman is a generation, a thing divine; in the living creature that is mortal it is something immortal' (*Symposium* 206c, using Irigaray's translator's translation).

This, for Irigaray, is the pivotal moment in the text. But it is one that, as she comments, 'never seems to have been heard'. This is because Diotima – or, Irigaray speculates, Socrates perhaps misconstruing Diotima – immediately goes on to two more familiar, and different, points. One is that what is immortal in procreative sex is the begetting of a child, in whom the parents' lives will continue after their death. The other is the invidious contrast Diotima (or Socrates/Plato) draws between heterosexual bodily love, which engenders children, and homoerotic spiritual love between men, which engenders wisdom and virtue. Procreation offers a taste of immortality, but it is inferior to the creation of spiritual truths and virtuous deeds which are genuinely immortal.

For Irigaray, Diotima's revolutionary insight into the immortality attaching to the act of heterosexual intercourse is betrayed by the double insistence that it yield offspring, and that its offspring are inferior to those of homoerotic unions. These two points of betrayal are due to the 'foundational act of meta-physics' which takes place in Plato's text alongside the anti- (or non-)metaphysical vision proper to Diotima herself. While Diotima (not coincidentally) already glimpsed this possibility of the sensible transcendental arising in the union of man and woman, the complementarity of sexual difference, its active fulfilment requires women to become autonomous so that they are genuinely complementary to men and not simply made in their mirror image. The sensible transcendental is most warmly alive in beauty, which, as Irigaray proposes, presumably meaning the beauty perceived by men in women and vice versa, embodies what is real in the fabric of the divine.

The creative mind: love and the power of art

Irigaray's conception of eros as sufficient in itself, the paradoxical conception of a sufficient intermediary, is an unorthodox one among readings of Diotima. More traditional is Iris Murdoch's emphasis on eros as a driving force which can move humans from egotistic obsession into the dimension of morality, so constituting a crucial element in the construction of an aspirational Plato. But Murdoch herself was unorthodox in distinguishing sharply between the role of (good) art and the erotic drives. This distinction is put to work in a Platonically inspired argument to defend art against the master himself, and so to explain the relative roles of art and love in helping humans to aspire to moral truth.

Nothing said so far about the *Symposium* or *Phaedrus* suggests that Plato had any hostility to art. But such hostility characterizes an aspect of the *Republic* which we have not yet mentioned. This is the famous fact that Socrates recommends censoring the poetry to be allowed into the ideal city, and ultimately recommends that the poets be banished from the city altogether. Inspired by the divine *mania* of the artist as portrayed in the *Phaedrus*, generations of artists, like Murdoch, have had to confront the fact that Plato, himself a peerless stylist and inventor of a new literary genre, seems in the *Republic* to condemn the poetic art. Murdoch's response was to defend the place of art in a Platonic universe – a universe in which the good is real though acting well is difficult – against Plato's own strictures against art. Like Wilde, Murdoch articulated her response by writing her own versions of Platonic dialogues, in her case with the added twist of including Plato himself as a character.

'Art and Eros' is one of a pair of dialogues which Murdoch published together as *Acastos* (1986), adopting Plato's custom of calling a work after the youth who is Socrates' main interlocutor. This dialogue, which was originally staged as a play in 1980, is between Socrates, Acastos ('a serious youth'), Callistos ('a beautiful youth', Mantias ('a political man in love with Callistos'), Deximenes ('a cynical man') and Plato. Each, except for Socrates, offers a definition of art. Art is sequentially defined as imitation, a tissue of falsehoods, rhetorical propaganda – but then the young and idealistic Acastos, appalled, interjects a clumsy definition of art as passionate insight into the world as it is. He is desperate to believe that 'goodness rests upon reality' – here is Nietzsche's foundationalist *bête noire* – and that art can be a true judge of the world and so be good for us and for society. Then Plato bursts in. Art, he urges, comes from the depths of our soul, from our eros or erotic passionate drive. Bad art is sheer selfish fantasy, a kind of pleasant masturbation. But good art is even more dangerous. Good art is an image of moral goodness. And because it is easier to watch a drama than to act rightly, good art is a distraction and a sacrilege. It tempts us away from trying for the real thing. 'Art,' says Murdoch's Plato, 'is the final cunning of the human soul which would rather do anything than face the gods.'[39]

Murdoch's own heart is clearly not with Plato, but with Socrates, whom she makes respond to his impassioned errant pupil. Socrates chastises Plato for assuming that we should be like gods, that we are not and should not be at home in our weak bodies and emotions which crave and respond to art. Says Murdoch's Socrates: 'Our home may be elsewhere, but we are not condemned to exile, to live here with our fellow exiles.'[40] Art is second-best to the gods, but it is the human best, and so the distinction between good art and bad art is critical. This is a distinction which Plato never made, but which Murdoch takes to be fundamental. Eros is the source of selfish fantasy, it is the source of bad art, so it cannot be the source of good art which in its essence is independent of our lusts and illusions. Good art is cold and objective and allows us to escape from the toils of the erotic.

A perfect example is found in Murdoch's novel *The Bell*. Dora, a silly and selfish young woman teetering on the verge of adultery, finds herself in London at the National Gallery. 'Her heart was filled with love for the pictures, their authority, their marvellous generosity, their splendour. It occurred to her that here at last was something real and something perfect. Who had said that, about perfection and reality being in the same place? Here was something which her consciousness could not wretchedly devour, and by making it part of her fantasy make it worthless.' Dora, the young woman, feels that she has had a revelation, and as she leaves, is buoyed by the hope that 'since, somewhere, something good existed, it might be that her problems would be solved after all'.[41] Murdoch counters the Nietzschean critique by adverting to a view close to that of Nietzsche's admired (though criticized) predecessor Schopenhauer, who had extolled art as a peaceful form of freedom from the relentless restlessness of will. Murdoch takes a more ethical slant than the contemplative Schopenhauer, but the vision of art as a source of emotional clarity and truthfulness is at work in her writing as well.

For Murdoch, the products of artistic creativity are admirable, somehow hallowed, while the murky workings of the creative imagination are more dubious: dangerous at best, destructive at worst. Before turning to the final piece of the aspirational puzzle, the role of the Good, consider some Platonizing accounts of the role of the imagination alternative to hers. The exemplar, tying imagination to recollection and both to moral and creative aspiration, is once again the one to be found in the fecund meditations of Coleridge.

The creative mind: imagination and recollection

It may be surprising to learn that even the 'geometric discipline' which we saw Coleridge to have admired in Plato can be understood as nourishing the imagination. The significance of geometry for the imagination was brought out a century after Coleridge by the French mystic and philosopher Simone Weil. Weil mused in her notebook: 'Teaching of geometry not as a sum of knowledge, but as a purification from error through imagination. Plato's procedure?'[42] Coleridge too saw the grasping of the world's intelligible structure as a function of the imagination. And he did so by invoking another characteristic Platonic doctrine, that of recollection.

3. Plato on Forms and Foundations

In Plato's *Meno* and *Phaedo*, the Socrates character conjectures that the human ability to learn is best explained as a faculty of recollection. He proposes that babies learn everything before birth (the doctrine is linked to a doctrine of reincarnation) but then forget it immediately upon being born. Learning is then a matter of remembering – 'recollecting' within one's own mind the truths once known. For Coleridge the idea of recollection was fertile because it ascribed a deep source of creative power to the human mind. Kant had tried to make the mind active, but his conception of the spontaneity of the understanding was narrower than Plato's. Coleridge's characteristic concern with explaining and vindicating the creative powers of the artist drew deeply from the Platonic well, using recollection to explain the powers of imagination. As a twentieth-century Platonist, a Christian professor at Princeton, would put it, 'the right use of the imagination is of the very essence of Idealism'.[43]

Coleridge, as we have seen, was as concerned as his younger contemporary Schopenhauer with explaining artistic creativity and its place in a created, seemingly causally determined universe. Schopenhauer would take the artist to be attaining contemplation of something divine. Coleridge saw the artist's creativity as activity rather than contemplation, yet still as linked to the divine. The constituting power of the mind resided in the 'primary imagination' which Coleridge described as the repetition in finite humans of God's eternal and infinite act of creation.[44]

In a post-Romantic age, the close bond Coleridge proposed between recollection and imagination may seem surprising. Is not recollection a matter of discerning what is already given, while imagination is a matter of inventing something new? Part of the answer lies in the broader sense of the term 'imagination' in Coleridge's day, following Kant's emphasis on the synthesizing faculty as itself creative. Another part lies in an aspect of the English Platonist tradition on which Coleridge drew.

In defending imagination and idealism, Coleridge was attacking the popular empiricist psychology he had studied as an undergraduate at Cambridge. But this battle between idealism and empiricism was a constant theme in English philosophical culture; a precursor had been fought two centuries before. At that time, in the seventeenth century, the disruptive empiricist challenge came from Thomas Hobbes. Hobbes, the 'beast of Malmesbury', had ravaged philosophy, propounding a thoroughgoing materialism in which there was no room for the immortal soul, no meaning to the word 'good' other than as a label for what the individual desires or the sovereign commands, no possibility of social peace without a sovereign to enforce it, and quite possibly no God (Hobbes was widely attacked as an atheist though modern scholars still debate his actual beliefs). It was against this kind of rabid challenge, and the new science which bred it, that a group of Anglican divines at Cambridge hoisted the Platonic flag, earning themselves the sobriquet 'Cambridge Platonists'.

While the views of the major members of the school (Ralph Cudworth, Henry More, John Smith and Benjamin Whichcote) differ in detail and in emphasis, it is the common elements which are most relevant to our theme. Plato had rightly taught, they argued, that humans pursue the good – that is, what they believe to be good. The pursuit of evil is explained as the result of a mistake made about the good. Goodness, therefore, has genuine motivating power. We have no difficulty knowing what virtue requires, which is the same as what our reason teaches: reason is, in Whichcote's famous phrase, 'the candle of the Lord'. And our moral understanding unites us to the mind of God. Here we find the Neoplatonist creed of the divine mind, which pervades the universe, incorporated into a Christian understanding. Plato's description of the Good as like the sun holds true also for God. Our eyes could not see the sun unless they were moved by the sun's power and form; so our souls could not see God unless God, who created us in His image, could be found and known within the self.[45] Morality is primary: this is what we are most securely able to know, by rational inquiry and introspection. (Strictly speaking, this composite Cambridge Platonist view may be neither transcendentalist nor foundationalist: although they believed that a transcendent God exists, they experienced the divine spirit as immanent in each soul and as imparting a knowledge of morality more fundamental than any metaphysical contention.) And because the rational ability to know this much is common to all, such morality can serve as a guide to social peace in a world riven by hostile creeds, as the third Earl of Shaftesbury would later influentially argue, drawing on these ideas.

The Cambridge Platonists did not actually endorse the full details of Platonic recollection, since that had involved the heresy of believing the soul to be (as the myths in Plato's dialogues suggest) reincarnated. But their view on the nature of learning and knowledge was similar, and explicitly indebted, to that of Plato. Learning, they believed, was a process of developing one's inner potential and innate ability to learn, an active endeavour of the sovereign mind rather than a passive reflection of the external world.[46] The Cambridge Platonists had no time for the attitude which Richard Rorty would later take to be characteristically (and fatally) Platonic – the idea of the mind as simply a 'mirror of nature'. It was the empiricists who saw mind as a passive mirror. The idealists and Platonists insisted otherwise: they celebrated the human mind as a divine creative spark.

Drawing on this tradition, then, as well as on Neoplatonism, Coleridge knitted together the several themes we have been exploring. Beauty, love, recollection, imagination: all these were Platonic touchstones which Coleridge imparted to his fellow Romantic poets and to the generation which followed. Wordsworth, who imbibed his Platonism from Coleridge, took the creative power of recollection as the explicit subject of his great poem, 'Ode: Intimations of Immortality from Recollections of Early Childhood' (1806). The Platonic theme has long been recognized in these famous lines:

> Our birth is but a sleep and a forgetting:
> The Soul that rises with us, our life's Star,
>   Hath had elsewhere its setting,
>   And cometh from afar:
>   Not in entire forgetfulness,
>   And not in utter nakedness,
> But trailing clouds of glory do we come,
>   From God, who is our home ...[47]

Shelley, Keats and others, as noted earlier, followed suit. And so, prefigured by the Cambridge Platonists and the sixteenth-century humanists, was founded a grand tradition of Platonism in English poetry. The burden of this tradition was that the creative power of art lay in the recollecting power of the mind. And not only art, but goodness, was the fruit of introspective memory. The theme of goodness is the last great theme in the aspirational Plato to which we must now turn.

Moral effort and the demands of the Good

Appeal to the Good (sometimes referred to as the 'Form of the Good') of *Republic* VI was a widespread strategy in the rehabilitation and improvement of Kant among Victorian, and contemporary German, scholars. In Marburg, in southwest Germany and in Oxford, the Kant-Plato nexus was at its closest. Indeed, although both the Marburg and southwest German schools have been dubbed 'Neo-Kantian', Hermann Cohen (Marburg) went so far with Plato as to declare that 'philosophy is Platonism', while his colleague Paul Natorp taught that Plato had travelled the same path as Kant from 'Dogmatism' through 'Scepticism' to 'Criticism' and so arrived at the modern Kantian truth of critical idealism.[48] But their reading of Plato was an extremely Kantian one. As this would come under attack by Heidegger and the Stefan George Circle (to be discussed in Chapter 4), it is important to remember that the Neo-Kantians were themselves on the attack, against a reading of Plato which they considered to be dogmatic (one might call it falsely foundationalist). This was the conception of the Ideas as a kind of vague reservoir of spiritual piety. Against this, the Marburg School launched their view of Plato as no dogmatic preacher, but a serious philosopher, an entirely correct predecessor of Kantianism.

Schopenhauer had treated the Ideas as prototypes. The Marburg School treated them as 'hypotheses', an unfortunate choice of term pilloried by the post-Nietzscheans, who saw this as a bloodless, subjective misunderstanding of the living power of Plato's Ideas.[49] The Marburg School never saw the Ideas as entities or substances, but rather conceived them in Kantian fashion, as modes of judgment or conditions of the possibility of experience. One commentator has noted that this reading of the Ideas was 'ontology-free'. In his later writings, Cohen, arguably the leading spirit of Marburg Platonism despite the fact that it was Natorp who in 1902 published a whole book on Plato, offered the clarification that the Ideas exist in the soul rather than in a dualistic realm of separate being. The dualist doctrine of the 'separation' of the Ideas, Cohen stated indignantly, was the false proposal of Aristotle, which made the Idea 'an utter matter of dogmatism'.[50] The Ideas enjoy 'true being', but this is not a matter of their having a separate being, rather, they are the true being of objects.

In ethics, Cohen adopted Plato's notion of the good as the object of our intention, our purpose (*Zweck*). As Plato had argued that all our pursuit of goods aims ultimately at the Good itself, so Cohen called God the 'Idea of the highest purpose', and identified this as the Good and as the principle of knowledge and of being. But Cohen, perhaps here encouraged by his Judaism which made him believe that some ancient cultures had held to higher ethical standards than others, believed that in Plato this identification of the Good had remained purely formal and empty, due to the state of development of Greek society in which slavery and privilege obscured the equality of human reason. Only in Kant had the content of reason as equal freedom been adequately recognized.

The reinterpretation of the Ideas, and the institution of the Good at the heart of a Kantian ethical programme, had also been carried out by the Oxford idealist movement a couple of decades earlier. Their common complaint was that Kant's ethical system was excessively formal and procedural. In focusing on the rational government of the will, he had ignored the question of the ends of action. T.H. Green, like Cohen, held that Kant's moral law would remain unintelligible and morally meaningless without the Platonic notion of 'an object unconditionally good', which would give meaning and direction to ethical striving.[51]

What Green meant was explained more fully in the writings of his friend and literary executor Richard Nettleship, also an Oxford don who devoted himself to lecturing on Kant and Plato. Both saw goodness as teleological (providing the ultimate purpose and explanation), a teleology reflected not in this or that particular object but in the intelligibility of the whole. Nettleship adopted Plato's *Repub-*

lic VI comparison of the sun as the condition of visibility, with the Good as the condition of intelligibility. As Nettleship put it, 'Intelligibility is the reflected light of the supreme person ... for a man to attain the good ... would be for him to live in the light.'[52]

Green and Nettleship made the centrality of goodness relevant to politics as well as art and ethics. They persuaded themselves and their disciples that an answer to the immoralists and political cynics could be found in the fact that the good was manifest in reality. Political ideals, in the ordinary sense of the term, are rooted in existing conditions even as they point beyond what is currently realized into the future. (A strong dose of Hegel here.) This guarantees the idealist against the charge of being a hopeless dreamer. Indeed it is the cynic, not the idealist, who on this account traduces the real. Iris Murdoch, again following this Oxford vein of Platonism, likewise insisted that goodness, as experienced in great art or in small deeds of kindness, reminds us that there is more to the world than our own selfish fantasies. To maintain this just perspective requires hard work and self-denial. But this alone is living in truth, in the light of the Good.

For Coleridge, goodness was rooted in introspection and memory. For Green, Nettleship and Murdoch, goodness is rather pictured in terms of attending to the call of something objective, and perhaps transcendent, from outside ourselves. (However, remember that part of the point of recollection is that these two paths may amount to the same thing.) Implicit in all these views is the final element in the aspirational Plato, one which is perhaps the least well known, but potentially the most significant for defending Platonism against the Nietzscheans. This is the idea that moral goodness requires serious, protracted, and sometimes painful moral effort. Although goodness is objective, becoming good or virtuous requires a lot of work with no guarantee. And as noted above, the idea of a guarantee is arguably at the root of what Nietzsche criticizes in Christianity. Let there be a rank-ordering of goodness, an elite of those who fashion themselves as moral agents, and much of the Nietzschean critique is pre-empted. It must be said at once that this need not be an exclusive elite. Plato based entrance to it on intellectual capacities, but Murdoch for example bases entrance to it exclusively on moral effort and self-awareness. The point is only that morality requires effort and aspiration; it is something people must work to achieve, not something which a priest or a simple act of belief can automatically achieve for them.

Consider a quotation from Paul Friedländer, the Plato scholar who in the 1920s moved toward the Stefan George Circle to be discussed in the next chapter. Friedländer's magisterial Plato book of that decade at one point seems to present a crudely visual and foundationalist account of the Forms, ascribing to Plato's Socrates the view that 'if there was such a thing as justice, if it was an Eidos [Form], then a person became just when he looked at justice'. But the continuation of the thought reveals that this is far from being the standard view marrying foundations to guarantees. Friedländer continues:

> 'Or do you consider it possible,' says Socrates in the *Republic* (VI, 500c), 'that a man would not imitate that with which he lives in admiring companionship? So the philosopher, in constant companionship with the divine order of the world, will reproduce that order in his soul and, as far as men may, become godlike.'[53]

The notion of 'imitation' is deeply Platonic; it characterizes the education recommended in the *Republic* on all levels, from the imitation of benevolent gods and courageous heroes by children, to the imitation of the Form of Goodness in their souls by the initiate-philosophers. The divine order of the world (its metaphysical structure) will not automatically reproduce itself in the human soul. Rather the aspiring philosopher must work hard to imitate and reproduce what he or she (remembering that Socrates in the *Republic* allows women into the ranks of the philosophers) admires.

Even if the Forms exist, whether transcendentally or immanently (for the sake of argument) providing a metaphysical basis for ethics, the soul's path to them does not run straight or smooth. The Forms must be internalized for them to achieve moral sway over our minds. And to do this requires a painful course of education as self-cultivation. Once this is acknowledged, it may be that much of the animus

95

underlying the Nietzschean attack on Plato as foundationalist will be defused. Indeed, whether or not Plato was a foundationalist matters less in light of this interpretation of what it would mean for him to have been one. If what matters is response to features of experience, aspiring to embody standards of goodness which impress one as apparent in it, the difference between a moral agent basing herself on a 'true' metaphysics and one basing herself on a false one may not make a difference to the practice of ethics. It is true that the language will differ – a language of discovery and insight, versus a language of creation and commitment – and Rorty would doubtless point out that on the Nietzschean view there is no basis on which the former language should be used. But to deprive the Nietzscheans of their easy dualist, foundationalist target, is to recall a Platonism which knows as much about the rigours of self-fashioning and the pleasures of the senses as they claim to do. And then, as Nietzsche himself suspected, the structure of belief may matter less than the moral imperative lying behind it. Consider the view advocated by Marcus Aurelius, the great Roman emperor and Stoic philosopher, who modelled his pursuit of duty based on reason on that of Socrates and his conception of wisdom on that of Plato: '... as to the whole, if God [exists] – all is well; if haphazard [i.e. if things are determined by chance], be not thou also haphazard' (*Meditations* IX, 28).[54]

4

The Political Plato: the First Totalitarian, the First Communist, the First Idealist?

Plato's pupils turned out to be dictators.   G.E.L. Owen[1]

Introduction

Owen was speaking of Plato's immediate pupils in the Academy. But his words apply to the twentieth century as well: socialists and fascists alike have invoked Plato to legitimate their programmes. Such invocations have divided their opponents: some attacking Plato for being eminently suited to such use, others claiming that the democratic or liberal Plato was being misinterpreted by the anti-democratic extremists. The litany of book-length attacks and defences in English alone is impressive. Attacks: Werner Fite, *The Platonic Legend* (1934); R.H.S. Crossman, *Plato Today* (1937); A.D. Winspear, *The Genesis of Plato's Thought* (1940); Karl Popper, *The Open Society and Its Enemies* (1945). Defences include two books published in 1953 alone: Ronald Levinson, *In Defense of Plato*, and John Wild, *Plato's Modern Enemies and the Theory of Natural Law*.

The immediate explanation as to how Plato is invoked by both Left and Right is straightforward. His *Republic* proposes radical means (a class of rulers who own no property and do not marry, whose procreation is strictly controlled, and who include both women and men in the naked exercises and philosophical study involved in being trained to rule) to achieve holistic ends: a society in which justice and harmony are achieved by making the citizens cohere as a unity, allowing (purported) natural inequalities to contribute to the greater good. The radical means have been celebrated by the Left, while the holistic goal of a citizenry shaped to be cohesive has appealed to the Right. Meanwhile, some self-proclaimed democrats have attacked the holistic goal as totalitarian, while others have argued that democracy too needs a holistic vision if it is to flourish.

As we saw in Chapter 2, the fortunes of democracy have changed dramatically since the American and French Revolutions. Once seen as a threat to governments, it became the battle-cry of governments fighting fascism. And this brought dramatic changes in the reading of Plato in its train. Once praised as the sensible enemy of democracy, in the 1930s and 1940s Plato was attacked as one of its most dangerous foes. Such indictments might hinge only on his affinity with dictatorship, as it were with the Right (epitomized by Nazi Germany). But they could also invoke his affinity with the radical programme of communism on the Left (epitomized by Stalinist Russia). While such exposés were being expounded in Britain and America throughout the 1930s and the war years, German writers had been invoking Plato as the educator and poet-legislator of a cohesive spiritual community from the 1920s onwards. From 1933, some of the proponents of these readings of Plato spurned National Socialism, while others merged their readings into its capacious and contradictory ideological flow. Some Anglophone opponents of Plato seized on the latter fact to bolster their case; Plato's defenders responded that he had been misused and abused by fascist propaganda.

This chapter focuses principally on the *Republic*, as made central to the understanding of Plato by Jowett in England, and as a key part of the Plato portraits developed in Germany in the early twentieth century. It begins with an account of those who saw Plato as a source of innocent moral-political inspiration, a supporter of a kind of idealistic status quo. In the second and third parts, those who found him a tribune of the communist Left, and those who opposed him as a reactionary anti-democrat, are considered. Here we observe the strange contrast between radical means and hierarchical ends. In the fourth part, we consider a different set of moral interpretations of Plato, this time as the cultural educator, or passionate poet-legislator-hero, which lent themselves to a politics impatient with the status quo, and in some cases eventually to fascism. In short, the polarized politics of the early twentieth century paralysed the understanding of Plato on all sides. Having surveyed the standoff over the political Plato in the modern period, we will turn in conclusion to compare this with earlier ways of learning from Plato in order to appreciate what has been forgotten and overlooked in the modern debates.

Before turning to these questions, it is useful to sketch the political dimensions of the *Republic* (without prejudice to the interpretative debates that inevitably arise, or to the other works of Plato which bear on his political theory). The *Republic* portrays the character of 'Socrates' trying to persuade Plato's two brothers that acting justly is genuinely beneficial to the individual and not to be avoided whenever one can get away with it. To show this, Socrates introduces a comparison between the psychology of an individual and the political structure of a city, which turn out to be closely intertwined. Each consists of three parts: the wise part (reason in the individual; philosopher-rulers in the city); the fighting part (spirited pride and anger in the individual; auxiliaries in the city), and the desiring part (appetites in the individual; ordinary people, farmers, artisans and merchants, in the city). Psychic health and civic health alike depend on the wise part being able to govern the other two, free from the danger of being overthrown by rebellion or undermined by resistance.

This requires strenuous education and discipline for everyone. For the rulers, it requires more: a philosophical higher education and an ascetic life without ties to property or family which could tempt them to pursue self-interest instead of civic happiness. The results are radically anti-conventional. The rulers are to live as a kind of super-family, having sex only on instruction and considering children to be common to all of them. Moreover, those women who are qualified are to act as rulers equal to the men. Chastity, monogamy and female subordination are all to be sacrificed to the unity of the ruling elite, a unity on which the broader unity of the city as a whole depends.

This virtuous, happy city is then contrasted with degenerate, imperfect cities. Among these, democracy ranks second to worst, better only than tyranny. In a democracy equality is the rule, rather than the hierarchy of reason, will and appetites which marks the good city. In a tyranny, the most vicious appetites rule, inverting the virtuous hierarchy and making reason their slave. The question whether the virtuous city is possible is debated at length. It is clearly impossible unless qualified philosopher-rulers can be found, but even then there are questions about how it could be established and whether it would be stable. Socrates says at one point that at least it can serve as a model, like the cosmic harmony of the heavens, for the individual to educate his or her own soul. Does Socrates mean that the city of the *Republic* could, or could never, be established? Does he mean his radical proposals about the rulers' property, family, and status of women to be taken seriously? To such questions, and their reception and implications, we now turn.

The *Republic* as moral inspiration for modern politics

A *reformist idealism*

Master of Balliol College and Regius Professor of Greek at Oxford, Benjamin Jowett introduced Kant, Hegel and Plato to the Oxford curriculum and integrated them into his emollient form of political idealism. In Jowett's case, 'political idealism' was specifically linked to his philosophical idealism (mentioned in the previous chapter), although in other cases 'political idealism' came to mean simply a vague programme of political hopefulness rather than any technical philosophical view.

Jowett conceived himself as fighting the latest round of the idealist-materialist battle, against materialist opponents who in his day were embodied by the utilitarian creed of Jeremy Bentham and his followers, J.S. Mill and George Grote. Utilitarianism held that the crucial test of any public policy was whether it served the greatest happiness. Jowett acknowledged that utility was important. But he argued that Plato's *Republic* showed that it was not enough. The highest law is not the greatest happiness, but the good and the right.[2] And that goodness was linked to God was something

Plato had taught and Christianity had confirmed (even though Jowett, especially in his younger days, was something of a religious radical). Thus Plato was enrolled to bolster the ethical dimension of political participation by all, including the elite, who aspire to intellectual excellence and moral rectitude.

So understood, Plato was the key source of inspiration for Jowett in his educational enterprise, described by one historian as 'the conscious creation of Platonic guardians for Britain and its empire'.[3] His students included Lords Curzon, Grey and Oxford (then Herbert Asquith), the future Archbishop of Canterbury Cosmo Gordon Lang, and the future Bishop Charles Gore. Florence Nightingale, who became a constant correspondent of Jowett's after her return from the Crimea, wrote to ask him whether a young soldier had been a pupil of his: 'He talks to his men about Plato & tells them they don't do what Plato would have them do, & don't realize Plato's ideal of what soldiers ought to be.'[4] As this quotation makes comically clear, Plato became a focal point of this programme of moral education for the elite. He was translated, mistranslated (as noted in Chapter 3 with reference to pederasty) and made consistent with the fundamental teachings of Christianity.

What Jowett found in Plato was not any kind of conventional, or specific, political programme. Plato's actual proposals, such as the equality of women rulers and communism of the rulers' property, were not to be taken seriously; in fact Jowett had proclaimed as sublimely irrelevant the question whether Plato actually considered his ideal to be possible. 'We have no need ... to discuss whether a state such as Plato has conceived is practicable or not ... For the practicability of his ideas has nothing to do with their truth.'[5] That was enough for Jowett and his students, living in the imperial sunshine, needing a moral basis for their commitment to reform and progress along the whole spectrum of liberal causes, without seeking a single set of doctrinaire political principles. When Jowett died, Florence Nightingale acknowledged that he had no clear positive doctrine, but insisted that his work as educator had no need for it: 'he did not feel, himself, the want of anything more definite, because as he always said: "The man is greater than the doctrine".'

As this eulogy shows, Jowett's political programme as derived from Plato remained vague. The younger Oxford men Richard Net-tleship and Bernard Bosanquet diverged from each other in developing it. All acknowledged that Plato had fallen short of the true Hegelian vision of the individual as 'the synthesis of the universal and the particular'.[6] Bosanquet, devoted to Hegel, never-theless interpreted Plato along lines as Hegelian as possible, as calling for a conscious level of organization of the whole society (an anticipation of what we will examine as his 'holism', below). Justice is not something to be imposed from without, but must emerge from the will of the community: 'Plato [did not] explain that Goodness means organization, co-operation, and strength.'[7] But the more liberal Nettleship feared that this ideal could be taken too far. Plato's proposed means (for the rulers) of communism and the abolition of the family, and his general aim of supreme social *esprit de corps*, could make sense in a moment of national crisis. Yet this is only half the truth about human nature, which is not capable of really leading a common life all the time. Nettleship took Plato's most important point to be not the forced achievement of national unity, but the education of individuals to exercise conscience and be united in their diversity. Social harmony was the right end, but the drastic abolition of the rulers' families should be substituted by making all families schools of unselfishness which could prepare citizens for serving the state.[8]

The niceties of disagreement between Bosanquet and Nettleship about Plato's liberalism did not prevent Plato from serving as a source of inspiration for Edwardian sociologists and liberals more generally, as the historian Jose Harris has observed.[9] And any doubts about the synthesis between Plato and Hegel were glossed over by Ernest Barker during the bloody upheaval of the First World War. While Bosanquet was attacked for being excessively, and illib-erally, Hegelian, Barker summed up the idealist Plato so as to leave no doubt of the Athenian's liberal credentials. Barker wrote in the first volume of his *Greek Political Theory* (1918) that although Plato had been wrong to separate reason from will and emotion in the psyche, he had rightly understood the significance of reason to the state. He had been wrong to sacrifice property, family and the domestic duty of women to his ideal ends. But Barker left no doubt in the reader's mind that Plato's ends had been genuinely ideal, and that they were aims which true liberals should still accept.

> It is certainly Plato's aim to destroy mere individualism, to abolish individual 'rights' as construed in the proposition 'might is right,' and to deny liberty in the sense of 'doing what one likes'. But ... it is as certainly his aim not only to guarantee but to develop individuality, in the true sense of the word, and with it the rights and the freedom it requires.[10]

The idealist Plato fostered moral reform and political harmony. As the political clouds of the 1930s began to gather, the call for the moral transformation that Plato could engender began to become more shrill, though its details remained vague. Writing in 1931, Goldsworthy Lowes Dickinson, whom we met in Chapter 3, called on Plato to provide a kind of spiritual and moral tonic to the self-interested tendencies of the time. Plato, wrote Lowes Dickinson, challenged the 'cultivated and efficient men of the world' of his own day, all the dull 'tories of Athens', in the name of the spiritual life which could transform politics if only one would hearken to it.[11] But Dickinson paired this standard idealist invocation with a rather more startling remark. Defending the idealist reading against charges of being dilettante or anodyne, he made a striking comparison: 'Plato was serious, as serious as the Bolshevists now are.' The comparison with the Bolsheviks, made also by Bertrand Russell, introduces the radical left-wing reading of Plato's politics, to be considered shortly.[12] But first we turn to the radical right-wing reading which posed Platonic idealism not as an inspiration to modern politics, but as a stark alternative.

A discontented idealism opposed to modernity

The view of Plato as a source of moral inspiration can cast a darker shadow on the status quo than the emollient idealists considered so far would suggest. We have been discussing writers who favoured liberal reforms within the existing political system, and who found in Plato the moral case and courage to pursue their ideals. But other writers have found Plato's ideal polity to pose a stark challenge to the conventional arrangements of the modern world. These are romantic anti-modernists, hostile to individualism and commercial society, who treat Plato as a symbol of a lost world of virtue and heroism.

A writer of the American South in the mid-twentieth century exemplifies this stance. Richard Weaver took an apocalyptic view of historical decline. He idealized the Middle Ages as a civilization governed on the Platonic terms of wisdom and virtue. 'The only source of authority whose title is unimpeachable at all times is knowledge.' Plato and Christianity agreed on the supremacy of virtue, and the humanist culture of leisure and learning had lived on in the antebellum American South. But already in the Middle Ages, according to Weaver, the rot had set in. 'The way was prepared for the criteria of comfort and mediocrity when the Middle Ages abandoned the ethic of Plato for that of Aristotle.' 'Comfort and mediocrity' became the values of the bourgeoisie, of the victorious North in the Civil War, and now of the modern world as such. Democracy and equality only indulge these bad instincts, and are hostile to the integrative development of character which is the duty of the gentleman.[13]

Condemning the 'foolish and destructive notion of the "equality" of the sexes', Weaver blithely ignored the equality of the women rulers proposed in the *Republic*. He likewise ignored the abolition of property for the rulers in setting out his own vision of small property holdings. His was not a Plato of the particular radical measures of the *Republic*, but an idealized Plato of moral rectitude, order and hierarchy, in short a Southern planter's Plato. For Weaver, Plato taught the virtues of a lost world, nostalgia for which cultivates an implacable dissatisfaction with the present.

More subtle was the dissatisfaction with modernity that characterized the complex thought of the German Jewish émigré Leo Strauss, who left Germany in 1933 and arrived in the United States after several years in England. After studying Spinoza and Hobbes, and having been deeply influenced by Nietzsche in his youth, Strauss came to the conclusion that politics and philosophy since Machiavelli had betrayed classical ideals for the sake of science, security and progress. But the relationship between politics and philosophy was itself far from simple. As he turned increasingly to Plato, led by his readings of the medieval Arab Platonists Alfarabi and Averroës, Strauss decided that Plato had seen that Socrates' public teaching (that the city's standards were merely conventional and not best by nature) had endangered both the city and himself. What Plato learned from Socrates' fate was that philosophers must shield the city from their full teachings in order to protect the city and themselves.

Strauss held that philosophers had to be ironical, like Socrates, in order to shield others from the offensive glare of their own superiority. They benefit the city mainly by protecting it against the corrosive realization that civic norms are merely conventional, not natural. This is true, but it is a truth which only the few, the philosophers, can bear to face. Knowing that the laws of the city could be otherwise, they know also that there is no way to establish a city which would fully satisfy the highest human aspirations. Those aspirations are met only in philosophizing, and that is an activity which turns away from the city even as it can be carried out only in the shadow of its pacific shelter. So Strauss taught his many and devoted American students a conservative politics of moderation, in order to free themselves for philosophy and simultaneously protect the city from fanaticism. Radical reform in the name of justice is impossible, and anyway would violate human nature, which cannot be satisfied by politics alone.

> Socrates makes clear in the *Republic* of what character the city would have to be in order to satisfy the highest need of man. By letting us see that the city constructed in accordance with this requirement is not possible, he lets us see the essential limits, the nature, of the city.[14]

For Strauss, therefore, the apparently radical politics of the *Republic* are a mirage: they are a product of the profound irony of the text. By ironically recommending institutions such as communal property, the abolition of the family and the equality of women for the ruling elite, Socrates (speaking for Plato) makes clear that radical politics is contrary to nature. Nature prohibits incest and prescribes property and inequality. The young gentlemen of Athens should respect natural limits rather than pursuing chimerical political ideals. It is not possible to assess this ironic reading of the *Republic* here.[15] Because no one considered in this chapter other than Strauss has taken such an ironic view, when reporting the *Republic* we will continue to do so as if the proposals made by Socrates were indeed intended to be taken seriously, since that is what the persons under consideration here did.

Radical measures: Plato's *Republic* as a textbook for communism and feminism

As we have seen, the anti-modernists ignored, or treated as ironic, the detailed political proposals contained in the *Republic* in favour of their general portrait of Plato as a teacher for gentlemen, while the Oxford idealists thought that the details need not be taken seriously so long as Plato's general commitment to a good society was imbibed. Perhaps the pessimism of the former as to whether their lost world could be regained, and the optimism of the latter about the status quo, converged in indifference to what Plato had actually believed could or should be changed in his own time. But in times of more radical upheaval, the quest to transform (or to resist the transformation of) the political world led to a new interest in the radical measures of the *Republic*.

Such interest is visible most strikingly in mid-nineteenth-century France. The question of what the revolution had meant, and of whether it should go farther – to bourgeois rule? to full democracy? to communism? and what of the Church in the face of secular republicanism? – was dynamite in the turbulent, suspicious atmosphere before and after the brief republican reprise of 1848. And in the controversy over communism in particular, Plato was at its heart.

The *Republic*'s teaching of a community of goods for the guardians had been generalized to all citizens in Thomas More's *Utopia* (1516) and linked to the story of the literal community among Christ's disciples in the adages of his friend Erasmus. In France, the terrifying spectre of communism (terrifying to defenders of any social system based on property) had been championed during the Revolution by Gracchus Babeuf, who had invoked Plato in his defence speech when on trial for his life. Among activists in the workers' clubs in the 1840s, the idea that Plato in his *Republic* had endorsed equality and communism became a rallying axiom of faith. Etienne Cabet's *Icarie*, describing a communist utopia, drew on his journalistic defences of Plato. And though less dominant, the theme of Plato's feminism – based on the demand for the equality of women guardians expressed in the *Republic* – also won defenders. The feminist and socialist Flora Tristan, for example, invoked Plato to defend the grievances set forward by the women's clubs and to demand emancipation.[16]

The comic stage was quick to caricature this popular picture of Plato. *La République de Platon*, a play that opened on 7 June 1848, was not a dramatization of the Greek text but a humorous fantasy about Plato's attempt to put it into practice. Plato was portrayed as an atheist republican club-member whose young wife decides to put his principles of wife-sharing into practice by having an affair with their neighbour. At the end Plato recants. This comic sally against the Greek philosopher was joined by a heavyweight effort by the philosophical establishment to re-impress the picture of an idealist Plato against the (in their view, false) communist Plato of the masses. Completed in 1840, Victor Cousin's celebrated translation of Plato into French had already showed sensitivity to the dangerous political implications of the *Republic*, in that it alone of all the dialogues was translated without any commentary. Now the revolution of 1848 showed that the danger was justified and might perhaps go even further. So counter-attacks against the radical popular readings of Plato were launched. Cousin's secretary Jules Simon attacked the communist fantasist Cabet, while the Academy of Moral Sciences published a series of pamphlets intended to teach the people about the eternal truths of idealist philosophy, in order to counter the evils of materialism, atheism and communism.

This regrouping of French philosophy against a subversive challenge had already begun during the 1840s. The philosopher Joseph Ferrari discovered this the hard way. A young lecturer of Italian origin, newly appointed to a post in Strasbourg, he began to lecture on the history of philosophy in the Renaissance. His expression of admiration for Plato's *Republic* was immediately attacked by Catholic auditors in a vilification soon joined by parts of the Paris press. Ferrari was suspended from his post, which he never recovered, his appeals falling on the deaf ears of the powerful Victor Cousin who advised ministers in these matters. In 1849, when Louis-Napoléon Bonaparte had been elected president (soon to make himself emperor), Ferrari attacked the 'salaried philosophers' of the French state for their submission to reaction and the Church and their betrayal of liberty and the republic.[17] As the radical novelist Stendhal had sensed as early as 1828, the danger was that the idealist, spiritualist philosophy championed by Cousin would serve to legitimize intellectual tyranny.[18]

The internecine struggles between Church and republic in 1840s France were similar in intensity to those brewing in the 1840s American South, hostile to Northern abolitionism. Again, in a context where radical political transformation – such as the curtailment or abolition of slavery – was a live possibility, the specific measures mentioned in the *Republic* won closer scrutiny. In the case of George Fitzhugh, the results of that scrutiny were damning. Fitzhugh attacked Plato as a seditious reformer, a kind of meddling Northerner, who wanted to abolish both the family (true, as we have seen, only for the ruling elite) and slavery (false: the abolition of slavery was not part of the *Republic*'s programme at all).

For Weaver, a century later and buffeted by nostalgia, Plato would be the hero of spiritual order and Aristotle the enemy standing for material progress. Fitzhugh put it precisely the other way round. For him, Plato was a subversive like the utopian communists Fourier and Owen, the abolitionist Greeley and the sophist Protagoras, about whom he wrote a dialogue. Aristotle in contrast defended in his *Politics* the benign patriarch of a household including natural slaves. Aristotle, and Athens, had understood the crucial role played by slavery in Athenian democracy and, by extension, in the American South. In Fitzhugh's polemical view, Plato had sought to subvert this sound and natural order with the instincts and goals of the political revolutionary.[19]

Anti-democratic ends: the idealist Plato
unmasked as a reactionary

In the previous section we looked at those who took the radical measures of Plato's *Republic* literally, whether as positive (the French workers) or as destructive (Fitzhugh). But even more common in the twentieth century, paradoxical as it may seem, were readings of Plato as a reactionary. These were driven by attempts to undermine the seeming otherworldliness of the idealist Plato considered earlier. Some Marxists sought to unmask Plato in this way rather than admire the *Republic*'s radicalism; more common were liberal democrats who in the heated atmosphere of the 1930s spurned the old idealist readings, seeking to unmask Plato not as a proto-liberal but rather as a proto-fascist.

Marxist unmaskings

To understand the strange juxtaposition of the communist Plato celebrated by the French workers on the one hand, and the Marxist historians' attacks on Plato on the other, one must remember the two faces of Marxism. A common understanding of Marxism restricts it to a straightforward political prescription: communism. This is what the French workers found in Plato, and what Bertrand Russell meant in comparing Plato with the Bolsheviks after the Russian Revolution. But Marxism also includes a theory of history which tries to explain why the prescription has not yet been fulfilled. In such accounts of history, the heroes are the materialist men of science and the 'revolutionary' class of that epoch; the villains include those who benefit from any given political set-up – the apologists, the rationalisers, the establishment.

In the early twentieth century, two English Marxists, one a historian (Benjamin Farrington) and one a literary critic (George Thomson), would cast Plato as just such a villain. For them, what counted in the *Republic* was not its recommendation of communism, which was in fact a retrograde form of communism, still relying on slavery (as in fact the text does countenance, despite what Fitzhugh believed). Plato's communism was 'parasitic' and 'backward', not progressive as real Marxist communism would be and so useless as a model for the latter.[20] What was central to the *Republic* was rather the fact that Plato endorsed an all-powerful elite, a 'ruling class', which he wished to keep in power, in the face of all the pressures for social progress, by resorting to ideological deception.

> It was to banish for ever the possibility of popular revolts and to establish a class-divided society on a secure basis that [Plato] sought to call in the aid of the governmental lie, and so to stamp it upon the soul of the people that they should be for ever incapable of questioning its truth.[21]

This resistance to the forces and voices of progress was what classed him irrefutably as a reactionary.

Some of the flourishes in these Marxist accounts were in turn unmasked by a spokesman for the liberal idealist Plato (and pillar of the Cambridge establishment), Francis Cornford. In an essay probably written during the Second World War, Cornford pointed out that the putative heroes of ancient Greek scientific enlightenment were really speculative and mystical philosophers. And he attacked the Marxist tendency to assume that the ideas of someone born into a class, as Plato was born into the Athenian oligarchy, can almost without exception be explained as defending that class. (The exception being the case of those who become Marxists.) Cornford claimed that if Plato had been an aristocrat in the traditional sense, 'he would have framed a constitution like the English squirearchy of the eighteenth century, instead of proposing a resolution which would have given Squire Western [comic stereotype of the country squire in Fielding's novel *Tom Jones*] an apoplectic fit'.[22] But Cornford did not mean that Plato had been a radical communist or subversive. No, he had been neither subversive nor ordinary elitist, but a meritocrat and genuine rational idealist. (When not confronting Marxists, Cornford could be more critical of Plato: in 1933, contrasting Plato with Socrates, he had compared Plato in the *Laws* to the Grand Inquisitor of Dostoyevsky's *Brothers Karamazov*, who would put even his teacher Socrates on trial.)

Cornford's essay was only published posthumously after the war, so did nothing to stem the tide of attacks on Plato which went on into the 1940s. The terms of his defence of democracy anticipated those which would be used in the Cold War, rather than being typical of the 1930s. Cornford's liberal commitments comported with a concern that democracy should not in practice exclude the superiority of the few best suited to rule: 'Plato was an oligarch and an aristocrat in the sense that he [implied: like any sensible politician] thought mankind can be well governed only by a few, and those few the wisest and the best.'[23] We will see that certain American writers of the 1950s, anxious about the materialism of the masses, would advance similar views, put starkly by Cornford as the claim that it is in practice an absurdity to suppose that one could find 'a democracy of rational equals' in any modern state. But such sociological frankness was in abeyance during the 1930s and 1940s, when the stark choice between democracy and fascism induced a generation of Anglo-Americans to expose Platonizing idealism as fostering the latter rather than, as for Cornford, the last of the idealists, supporting the former.

Liberal unmaskings

As we have seen, generations of idealists had held Plato's moral teachings to be compatible with Christianity. Werner Fite, a Princeton colleague of one of the most vocal American idealists, Paul Elmer More, had no patience with this view, which he saw as so much drivel. The idealists – Ernest Barker and Bernard Bosanquet, as well as A.E. Taylor, the American scholar Paul Shorey and others – had eulogized a Plato who supported public education and promoted an idealist system of true liberty. Fite's comment on them was sarcastic.

On the surface Plato's republic is a simple military autocracy designed to mold the character of its citizens in accordance with a preconceived model of perfection: in reality – we are now to see [as the idealist Ernest Barker had argued] – it is a plan for realizing individual liberty, based upon a tender respect for true personality.[24]

111

Plato's republic, according to Fite, was no such thing. Fite pointed out that all the interesting prescriptions of education and even communism were designed only for the rulers. Plato was indifferent to the welfare of the 85 per cent of the citizens who would not be rulers, and he was willing to let them be fooled by the audacious propaganda of the 'noble lie' into believing themselves to be naturally inferior and to belong to the city. In ignoring the many, he had betrayed the great cultural achievements of Athenian democracy, dreaming instead of the elitist virtues of barbaric Sparta. He was no proto-Christian, but a true pagan, with only useless or pernicious moral teaching to offer. Nor did Fite have any patience with the 'Socrates yea, Plato boo' school of argument which we met in Chapter 2 and which has found so much favour since the Enlightenment. Socrates, he held, had fought for no cause greater than himself, certainly not for free thought or free speech. Neither Socrates nor Plato had defended democratic politics or anything like it, and there were no grounds for their spurious canonization as the patron saints of Western freedom.

The next sally against the idealists' Plato came ironically enough from Oxford, the onetime bulwark of idealism. And it came from Richard Crossman, later to be M.P. and minister in Wilson's Labour government, whom we have already met in Chapter 2 defending Socrates instead of Plato. Crossman announced in Oxford in 1937 that the idealist reading was – like so much else – a casualty of the Great War. Before the war, the *Republic* could be idealized as the perfect state, the beautiful but remote and irrelevant fancies of a dream. Now, however, faced with the ideological clashes of the 1930s, Crossman suggested that it was finally evident that Plato's purported 'idealism' had really been pure 'realism'. Plato had been if anything too realistic about the moral and intellectual capacities of the masses, the usefulness of dictatorship as a bulwark against class-war and communist revolution, the merits of propaganda as a tool of government. Now Plato could at last be rightly understood not as proposing a liberal chimera, but as a tough politician offering the strict dictatorship that might (so many thought) be needed to ward off communism and repair the hypocritical failings of democracy. Crossman addressed himself to people who might be asking:

112

' "Perhaps we have been building on foundations of sand. The ideals of freedom and democracy are crumbling away. Is it not better before it is too late to replace them with the Platonic 'dictatorship of the best'?".'[25]

Crossman sought to show that any such hope was a cruel and dangerous illusion. He admitted that Plato's toughness had not been simple thuggery. Plato had wanted to combine the discipline and unity of Sparta with the philosophical reason of Athens and Socrates, and to do this in a state which would genuinely make each citizen happy. This was not sheer class politics, but rather an attempt to make sense of the prejudices of his class by transforming them into a philosophical ideal. 'Plato dreamed of a civilized Sparta in which the serfs would be subjects, voluntarily submitting to the rule of law, not slaves terrorized by a secret police.'[26] Nevertheless, that dream was impossible, and so dangerous, for reasons still applicable in the 1930s:

> The *Republic* is ... a solution of the problem of government which could only be successful if men were not what they, in fact, are. Granting to the aristocratic elite absolute freedom of action, it demands of them a virtue far beyond their reach: demanding of the lower orders absolute obedience, it denies to them any possibility of self-realization. It makes the former divinity incarnate, the latter humanity with only a tiny spark of the divine. For this reason it is no surprise to discover the Platonic ideal realized in the structure of the Catholic church. Substitute the clergy for the philosopher-kings, and the laity for the civilians, and you have the one practical fulfilment of the Platonic programme. But in the field of government, Platonism, because it is at once too ideal and not ideal enough, becomes the rational apologia for reaction.[27]

Plato's dream of a 'dictatorship of the virtuous right' would be acceptable neither to the workers nor to the rich. It could be imposed only by military dictatorship, which would then end up serving the interests of the oligarchy who ran it. It would inevitably become 'a polite form of Fascism'.[28]

113

This conclusion meant that Platonic politics could not provide the conservative, undemocratic alternative to Hitler that some well-meaning but deluded English and French were seeking. But Crossman was aware that some Germans were meanwhile calling directly on Plato as providing grounds to support Hitler. This Crossman could not accept. In his view, Plato's intention was never to denigrate reason nor to worship power for its own sake, even though in practice his politics would unwittingly but inevitably lead to fascism.

The conceit of Crossman's book is that he introduces Plato to contemporary societies (Britain, Soviet Russia, Nazi Germany) and imagines what he would have to say about them. In Nazi Germany his Plato meets an imagined German academic who since 1933 has been a supporter of Nazism and written his great work, 'Platon und der Ursprung des Nationalsozialistischen Staatsgedankens' ('Plato and the origins of national-socialist political thought'). The German is delighted to meet Plato, whom he so much admires and believes will approve of his work and his Party. But Plato tells him off. He may have admired Sparta, he tells the startled German, but he can have no truck with the worship of power for power's sake or the attack on reason. After all, he was still the pupil of Socrates.

We will return to Crossman's German academic, and find that he may not have been so very imaginary after all.[29] But for now, we should observe that Fite and Crossman concentrate their fire on the political import of Plato's project. For all their differences (Crossman, for example, being more sympathetic to Plato's intentions), they agree on what they take to be the basic facts of the case. The *Republic* is anti-democratic; it is anti-egalitarian; its projected ideal state will inevitably succumb to the forces of ordinary dictatorship. But the most famous attack on the political Plato, the only one still widely read today, expands on the indictment. Karl Popper, in *The Open Society and Its Enemies* (vol. I: *The Spell of Plato*; vol. II, *The High Tide of Prophecy*, is about Hegel and Marx), charged Plato with being not merely anti-democratic, but also perniciously utopian. Plato's fundamental error was in believing that society could be engineered along utopian lines at all; the particular lines he chose, and their errors, are secondary to this fundamental illusion.[30]

Crossman wrote in 1937, in the wake of the Great War and in the

114

throes of the Great Depression and the rise of Fascist forces in Italy, Germany and Spain. In exile in New Zealand from March 1937, Popper later dramatically recalled that he decided to write the book on the day the Germans marched into Austria, and finished it in 1943. As his pairing of Marx with Plato shows, he was already thinking in terms of communism and fascism as inspired by similar forms of historicism and totalitarianism. (Crossman had treated the two extremist regimes quite separately, although George Orwell among others had painfully learned their similarities in Spain.) Popper's critics would call his thesis that of the totalitarian Plato, although Popper himself preferred the terms, borrowed from the French philosopher Henri Bergson, of the opposition between 'closed' societies and the 'open society'.

Closed societies, according to Popper, are hierarchical and do not tolerate dissent from their authoritarian world views; communism and fascism are only the most recent and technologically developed examples. The open society (in the singular: all happy open societies are alike, all unhappy closed societies are different) is a rare and fragile achievement. It was born in Greece under the 'Great Generation' of Pericles. It is organized democratically, and this means above all not this or that electoral device, but the fundamental freedom of thought and speech which (as Popper argued in his philosophy of science) is indispensable to the advancement of knowledge.

For Popper, as we saw in Chapter 2, Socrates had been a loyal subscriber to the open society, even though aspects of his thought could be pushed in dangerous directions. Plato, in contrast, belonged to a small, bitter circle of Sparta-loving aristocrats who wanted to turn back the evolutionary clock. They wanted to restore the closed society and erase the norms of reason, criticism and equality. Popper insisted that Plato was essentially looking backwards, aware that Athens had degenerated and seeking somehow to put things right. Plato was a kind of anti-modernist himself. Yet he was not the happy inhabitant of a virtuous community *à la* Weaver, but rather a revolutionary-reactionary who knew that heroic measures were needed if justice and happiness (as he understood them) were ever to be restored.

115

Popper's argument can be summed up by the two quotations which he placed as epigraphs on the first page of his volume on Plato.

For the Open Society (about 430 B.C.):
> Although only a few may originate a policy, we are all able to judge it.
>
> PERICLES OF ATHENS

Against the Open Society (about 80 years later):
> The greatest principle of all is that nobody, whether male or female, should be without a leader. Nor should the mind of anybody be habituated to letting him do anything at all on his own initiative; neither out of zeal, nor even playfully. But in war and in the midst of peace – to his leader he shall direct his eye and follow him faithfully. And even in the smallest matter he should stand under leadership. For example, he should get up, or move, or wash, or take his meals ... only if he has been told to do so. In a word, he should teach his soul, by long habit, never to dream of acting independently, and to become utterly incapable of it.
>
> PLATO OF ATHENS

The contrast makes Popper's argument clear. Plato wanted to replace the open society of democratic Athens with a closed one, or more precisely, to restore the closed society of the past in which aristocrats had ruled and discipline had reigned, as he believed was still true of Sparta. In the last chapter of the book, Popper admitted that Plato's intentions may have been genuinely to produce happiness – as he understood it – for the citizens, and acknowledged that Plato had a genuine hatred of tyranny. But the very aspiration to reform society on so gigantic and comprehensive a scale remained his fundamental mistake.

Such an aspiration was an example of what Popper called 'utopian social engineering'. This involved viewing society as a gigantic experiment which the experimenter could redesign starting from scratch. One form, characteristic of Plato, was to turn politics into a kind of aesthetics. 'The Platonic politician composes cities, for beauty's sake.'[31] Yet all such approaches run the overwhelming risk of going wrong. One never has a fully blank slate, one never knows the unintended consequences of each new radical idea, not to mention the temptations of corruption which afflict all rulers. Plato's project risks all on an adequate answer to the question, 'Who should rule?' But this, said Popper, is wrong and deeply misleading. The real question, and one which demands a democratic answer, is 'How can we so organize political institutions that bad or incompetent rulers can be prevented from doing too much damage?'[32]

Popper's scholarship was immediately questioned. For example, the shocking epigraph attributed simply to 'Plato of Athens' above is in fact from Plato's *Laws* (942c-d), from a context describing military discipline. (Popper assumed the compatibility of the *Republic* and the *Laws*, something we cannot discuss here but which must at least be scrutinized.) But the fundamental point of his objection was on his own terms sound. Plato did not value democracy, nor the everyday notion of liberty as freedom to do what one pleases, as necessary to the ideal city. Yes, he wanted to engineer a state to make all citizens happy, but only on condition that all submit to the rule of reason which some would have to prescribe to others. And the impact of the book, published in London in 1945, far outstripped the fate of Plato alone. One classicist, though mildly critical of Popper's scholarship, enthused that the book announced 'the political and moral values for which the free world will fight'.[33]

In the 1950s, however, the terms of Popper's defence began to be questioned. Other liberals grew anxious to enrol Plato again among their own ranks rather than sacrifice him to their opposition to totalitarianism. Moreover, Popper's defence of democracy could seem morally hollow. Not any one moral value, but the tolerance of moral debate, was for him the real democratic foundation. For a new breed of democrats this was unsatisfactory. The free world needed positive values for which to fight, not an empty allegiance to freedom of speech.[34] And several writers turned to Plato to supply those positive values, against a godless communism which was perhaps the real home of relativism. The editor of a volume entitled *Plato: Totalitarian or Democrat?* summed up the rival views.

(1) A supporter of democracy who holds that values are relative will see democracy as moral relativism in practice and totalitarianism as moral absolutism in practice. [Popper]
(2) A supporter of democracy who holds that values are absolute will see democracy as moral absolutism in practice and totalitarianism as moral relativism in practice. [Popper's critics: new Cold War view][35]

On both views it could be agreed that Plato was a moral absolutist. But whereas on (1) he appears as an execrable totalitarian-in-training, on (2) he could be seen instead as an admirable democrat. Plato now stood for absolute natural rights against the corrupting moral scepticism of the ancient Greek sophists and modern-day existentialists. This was essentially a new and improved model of the idealist Plato. The old kind, with its Hegelian affinities and hankerings after the organic state, had been discredited in England by the general revulsion against German philosophy. The new model Plato was a moral dogmatist, a defender of the fundamental value of human dignity and equality which had blossomed in Judaism and Christianity. The idealist Plato was no longer safe from the cut and thrust of mundane politics as had been the case in the halcyon days at Balliol. Now the idealist Plato was just another conscript in the ideological wars.

Plato as moral inspiration revisited: Weimar Platos and their progeny

The original, Oxford-issue, idealist Plato was, as we saw, a political one, but political only in the vague sense of supporting moral commitments to reform. The spiritual and aesthetic values of the English Romantic and poetic Platos whom we met in the previous chapter perhaps tempered any tendency to find Plato objectionable. Even Crossman found something to admire in Plato; the most uncompromising attacks on the Greek in English came from America or from Popper in New Zealand.

Germany, in contrast, had no strong tradition of the political Plato until the twentieth century. It had had its neo-Kantianism, but whereas English idealism had linked Plato to Kant and Hegel in describing an organic, or at least interdependent, political community, German neo-Kantianism had shunned Hegel and linked Plato with Kant for epistemological and metaphysical purposes only. Paradoxically, it was Friedrich Nietzsche who pointed the way to young Germans eager, in the early twentieth century, to escape from the dry tutelage of the neo-Kantians and to reconnect (as they put it) thought with life, reason with will, the soul with the body. We met Nietzsche's strictures on Platonism as dualism and proto-Christianity in Chapter 3. But there was also another, less obvious side to Nietzsche's view of Plato, upon which the new generation seized. Consider this passage from *Daybreak* (1887):

'The evil principle.' Plato has given us a splendid description of how the philosophical thinker must within every existing society count as the paragon of all wickedness: for as critic of all customs he is the antithesis of the moral man, and if he does not succeed in becoming the lawgiver of new customs he remains in the memory of men as 'the evil principle'. From this we may gather what the city of Athens, tolerably free-minded and avid for innovation though it was, did with the reputation of Plato during his lifetime: is it any wonder if, filled with the 'political drive' as he himself says that he was, he attempted three times to settle in Sicily, where at that time a Pan-Hellenic Mediterranean city seemed to be in process of formation? In this city, and with its help, Plato intended to do for the Greeks what Mohammed later did for his Arabs: to determine customs in things great and small and especially to regulate everyone's day-to-day mode of life. His ideas were surely *practical* as those of Mohammed were practical! A couple of accidents more and a couple of accidents fewer – and the world would have seen the Platonization of the European south ... But success eluded him: and he was thus left with the reputation of being a fantasist and a utopian – the more opprobrious epithets perished with ancient Athens.[36]

Here Plato is portrayed as having lusted for power – the power to

119

institute a new kind of regime which would educate, discipline and transform human souls. Plato is considered as a potential spiritual lawgiver, like Mohammed or Moses. But whereas they are admired as great religious founders, he has been considered no more than an idle dreamer only because of the contingent fact that his laws were never established. This, says Nietzsche, was not for want of trying. In describing Plato's three voyages to Sicily, he is following the *Seventh Letter*, the authenticity of which occasioned great debate among nineteenth-century German philologists. This letter, if it is by Plato, gives his autobiography with an emphasis on the political dimension. Plato had initially expected to enter politics, as befitted his high birth and powerful family connections. But he was disillusioned with democracy by the death of Socrates. His years of study taught him how a virtuous community could be established and governed, and he sailed three times to Sicily to advise two successive tyrants and concert with a more liberal friend and would-be ruler there. Political ambition is thus shown to be a crucial aspect of Plato's life and work.

It was this Plato, the ambitious and aspiring lawgiver, to whom the interwar generation in Germany quickened in reading Nietzsche. Like Wilde and Pater, the aesthetic modernists in Britain a few years earlier, they had no time for the old dualist shibboleths, even those propagated about Plato by Nietzsche himself. This new German Plato offered 'not a denial, but an affirmation' of the body; even the *Phaedo*'s stark contrast between the mortal body and immortal soul was read not as a dualist transcendence of body by soul, but rather as affirming the way that soul animates and permeates body.[37] But unlike the Plato of Wilde and Pater, who was an aesthete rather than an idealist politician, this new German Plato combined art, will, body and politics in one powerful and sinuous affirmation.

To be more precise. In fact several versions of this Plato sprang up, each engaged in bitter internecine warfare against the others. Ulrich von Wilamowitz-Moellendorff, the grand old man of German philology, produced a biographical study of Plato in 1919 which made much of the *Seventh Letter* and the political dimension. Werner Jaeger, who had been his student, meanwhile was developing his programme of the 'Third Humanism', in which Socrates and

Plato were enlisted as great educators who had helped to shape Greek culture (exercising what Jaeger called *paideia*, roughly equivalent to the German *Bildung* or education, by bringing out a student's inner capabilities and giving them shape and individual expression). This programme combined philosophy, inequality and politics in a potent way. As Jaeger wrote in the first volume, published in Germany in 1933 and republished in 1935 (although for the sake of his second wife, who was half-Jewish, Jaeger would leave for America in 1936):

> [The aristocrats] Pindar and Plato never fell under the democratic illusion that reason can educate the masses. Socrates, the commoner, rediscovered the old aristocratic distrust of universal education. Remember the profound resignation of Plato's seventh letter ... in which he speaks sadly of the narrow limits which bound the influence of knowledge upon the masses, and of the reasons which led him to address a small audience, rather than preach the gospel to the multitude. But remember also that despite their doubts it was the intellectual aristocrats of Greece who founded and formulated all the higher culture of the nation; and you will realize that the eternal greatness and fertility of the Greek spirit were created by that conflict between the will to educate and the disbelief in the possibility of universal education.[38]

Jaeger had already linked his humanism to a revanchist politics in a 1924 speech commemorating the founding of the Second German Empire, and in other writings he advanced a picture of Pericles, for example, as a *'Führer'* which was consonant with calls for such a leader being expressed by those openly or covertly dissatisfied with Weimar democracy.[39] But there was something stuffy about Jaeger's programme which made it vulnerable to that of another group keenly reclaiming Plato in not dissimilar terms: the followers of Stefan George.

The George Circle cordially loathed Wilamowitz, not least because of his youthful attack on Nietzsche's *The Birth of Tragedy*. Their relations with Jaeger were uneasy; some members of George's and Jaeger's circles overlapped, but the two movements were not really in sympathy. And it was the George Plato who came to pose the most significant challenge to that of Wilamowitz: as a recent commentator has put it, Wilamowitz's picture of 'Plato the man' succumbed to the George Circle picture of 'Plato as *Gestalt*', as a 'timeless heroic figure'. *Gestalt* was a favourite George Circle word, evoking feeling, idea and will as a pulsing unity.[40]

Stefan George was a great poet, widely seen in his day as the only real rival to Rilke; a brooding, magnetically attractive, homoerotically inclined man who drew the cream of German youth into his circle of passionate intellectual and emotional intercourse. George rejected the austerities of Kantian and neo-Kantian morality, according to which one acts rightly by following a universal law. Instead, with Nietzsche, he urged that what nourishes human growth is not formal law but the forceful example of a hero, the bearer of a powerful will. Only a hero could teach others to see with new eyes, could shape them into vital and healthy forms of aspiration and achievement. The way that a hero seized the moment in imposing will and vision established for each lesser mortal, in the words of George's disciple Friedrich Gundolf, 'a responsibility, a demand and a standard'.[41] The idea which captured this image was that of the 'founder'. The hero was a founder, a founder of a new way of seeing, of writing, at the highest level a new way of acting.

George's acolytes plunged into the task of portraying such heroes. They included great artists (Raphael, Holbein); great heroes of action (Napoleon, Frederick II, Caesar); and great poets (Hölderlin, Kleist, Goethe, George himself, and Shakespeare, as well as the founders of new cultural visions of art such as Burckhardt and Nietzsche). Once he had been highlighted by Kurt Hildebrandt's 1912 translation of the *Symposium*, Plato became a favourite of this kind. This was because he could embody all three types – artist, hero, philosophical and political founder – in an indestructible unity. Socrates, on the other hand (and in stark contrast to the English case), never captured the Circle's imagination. He was seen mainly as a rather ineffective precursor to Plato, the herald but not the king. It was Plato who both announced and (in his Sicilian adventures) embodied the dazzling model of a philosopher-king, an intellectual who sought and wielded power to shape men's minds. Concerns with the soul, with the erotic drive, with the cultural and intellectual leadership exercised by great men, all characterize George Circle discussions generally and discussions of Plato in particular.

The cultural impact of the George Circle was dramatic and widespread. Traditional scholarship was affected: Paul Friedländer wrote to his teacher, the scholar Wilamowitz-Moellendorff, that he had found a new path thanks to Heidegger, George and Nietzsche (though Friedländer remained torn between his two allegiances, dedicating a book conceived in George Circle terms to Wilamowitz).[42] The Neo-Kantians and their Platos were deserted. Natorp revised his own book on Plato to take account of the new concern with soul and eros; Heinrich Friedemann, one of Natorp's students, gravitated towards George and his friend Wolfskehl and published the passionate *Platon. Seine Gestalt* with their press in 1914. Kurt Singer, Edgar Salin, Kurt Hildebrandt and others wrote on Plato with George's approval and interest. This Plato was not the foundationalist whom Nietzsche and Heidegger had criticized as a misguided dualist. On the contrary, according to the George Circle Plato was himself the man of will and authenticity of whom they, like Nietzsche and Heidegger, dreamed.

George's last collection of poetry, published in 1928, was called *Der Neue Reich* (*The New Kingdom*). He spoke often of a 'secret Germany' whose prophet and poet-founder he with his disciples would be. Plato too was described as the 'founder', 'leader' and 'ruler' (*Gründer*, *Führer*, *Herrscher*) of a new realm. To speak of a *Führer* and of a new *Reich* in the late 1920s and early 1930s was, and is now for the historian of the period, to beg an enormous question. What was the political stance of the George Circle Plato?

In answering this one must note two things. The first is that the cultural influence of the George Circle Plato (and so its potential political implications) went far beyond that of the work of George's actual intimates. The second is that the post-1933 political bent of accounts of Plato influenced by George Circle views, like the post-1933 political views of the Circle's members in general, diverged dramatically. George himself died before making his views on the new regime unambiguously clear. Hitler was elected on 31 January 1933 and George never returned from his vacation in Switzerland that summer, dying in Locarno in December. True, he had refused to allow the Nazis to establish a Stefan George prize for young poets, and had refused the presidency of the *Dichterakademie* (Academy of Poets). But the terms of his refusal and of other comments on the regime were too ambiguous to determine the alignment of his followers once and for all. And so the Circle split. Some flattered or joined the Nazis, much like Crossman's imagined, but perhaps not so fanciful, Nazi Plato-scholar.[43] Others objected, fled, or resisted.

Consider, in the first category, a book published in 1933 by Kurt Hildebrandt, who had become close to George after publishing the 1912 Plato translation mentioned above. In this book, *Der Kampf des Geistes um die Macht* (*The Struggle of the Spirit for Power*), Hildebrandt expressed views common to many of the Circle's works on Plato. He attacked Natorp's abstract logical account of Plato, appealed instead to the 'creative power' of Plato's 'political will', and celebrated the indivisible unity of 'will and action' and Plato's '*Führergedanken*' (leadership thinking).[44] And in an afterword he adverted to an aspect of Plato's politics which became crucial to the Nazi wing of the Circle and those influenced by them.

This is the prescription in the *Republic* that the rulers should engage in eugenic breeding (*Republic* 460a-461c). Freed by the abolition of the family among their own ranks, they can prescribe the best pairings to ensure healthy and philosophical offspring; careful to watch the lower orders, they can eliminate a vicious or ungovernable child by exposure after birth (a common Greek practice). Hildebrandt, writing in 1932, picks up this aspect of the text with approbation:

That Plato is the founder of eugenics theory has already been pointed out by the spokesman of the German race-hygiene movement. I have in *Norm und Entartung des Staates* [*Normality and Degeneration of the State*] and in *Staat und Rasse* [*State and Race*] described Plato as the model for the bodily and spiritual effects of eugenic cultivation and the spiritual state.[45]

124

Now it is important to acknowledge that to endorse eugenics even in 1932 was not necessarily to express National Socialist sympathies. An incidental passage from one of the postwar defences of Plato shows that in 1953 such endorsement was still acceptable in liberal American circles. Trying to refute Popper's charge that Plato's interest in eugenics proves him a 'racialist', John Wild argued that 'it would be absurd to bring the charges of racialism against all those in democratic countries who now favor sterilizing certain criminal types'.[46] But the 'spokesman of the German race-hygiene movement' to whom Hildebrandt refers is not someone whose politics can be in doubt. It is Hans F.K. Günther, described by Walter Kaufmann as 'the Nazis' greatest race authority', whose 'tracts on race sold hundreds of thousands of copies in Germany and went through several editions even before 1933'.[47] Among the literally dozens of books Günther wrote about race was one on Plato's purported views of the subject (anachronistically inferred from his views on eugenics and on non-Greek 'barbarians'). Günther was not a member of the George Circle. But his book on Plato shows how far their characteristic formulations had entered the vocabulary of available and familiar cultural criticism.

Günther explains that by calling Plato a philosopher he means not that he is a logician or epistemologist (the familiar jibe at Natorp and company) but that he is a *'Denker'* (thinker: a George-type term), who seeks not objectivity but the accomplishment of a purpose. Plato had understood the profound teaching that *'die Philosophen sollen die Führer sein'* (the philosophers should be the rulers). And despite his relative lack of advanced racial science, Plato had firmly grasped the prior proposition that *'Menschen reinen Blutes sollen allein philosophieren'* (only men of pure blood should philosophize).[48] This shows how readily the language of the Circle, and in particular those discussions linked with wider interest in the eugenicist side of Plato, could be adapted to Nazi ends.

The same point can be made by considering another book, written before 1933 but, according to its author, welcomed by a publisher only in that year. Joachim Bannes wrote *Hitlers Kampf und Platons Staat* (*Hitler's Struggle and Plato's State*) as an appendix to a broader study of Plato but published it separately in 1933 because

125

it set out the ideological framework of the National Socialist 'freedom movement', as stated in its subtitle. Again, the book shows clear traces of George Circle vocabulary even though Bannes had no direct connection with any of its prominent members. He proclaims that for Plato, freedom and the Ideas are united in the heroic *Gestalt* of Socrates' eros for the whole, using George Circle vocabulary though giving more credit to Socrates than they normally did. Plato is a hero of inner cultural and national action and is to be compared with Schiller, Goethe and Shakespeare as heroes of German poetry (it had long been common for Germans to consider Shakespeare an honorary German author). Bannes insisted that Hitler and Plato both believed that only individuals, not the anonymous masses, can be truly responsible, and that both held a conception of politics which is extraordinarily distinct from the political life of everyday parties. (National Socialism at this time made much of being a dynamic 'movement' rather than a conventional 'party'.)[49] The enthusiasm Günther and Bannes showed for Plato was confirmed in the principal Nazi ideological-philosophical manifesto, Alfred Rosenberg's *The Myth of the Twentieth Century* (1934). Rosenberg praised Plato as an aristocrat who had represented the true admirable features of Hellenism, but excoriated the Socratic elements in him.[50] School textbooks compiled for Greek classes all over Germany soon reflected this same approbation.[51] While the interest in Plato went beyond the George Circle, their reading had a deeper and wider influence than has been hitherto acknowledged.

But not all those influenced by the George Circle drew National Socialist conclusions from their tenets. We conclude with the case of someone who was manifestly influenced by the Circle's thought but remained an outsider, using its language for his own ends. The Viennese legal scholar Hans Kelsen published two important articles on Plato in 1933, leaving Austria for America just as they appeared in print.[52] In the one on justice (a theme which would preoccupy him throughout his career), he paid tribute to 'the new Plato research' for having destroyed the idea that Plato was a theoretical philosopher aiming to found a pure science and having shown instead that Plato was rather a 'politician, educator and founder' driven by the imperative to rule others.[53] In case there was any doubt about which new research he meant, he named the books on Plato written by Edgar Salin (1921) and Kurt Singer (1927), both of whom belonged to the George Circle. Kelsen noted wryly that Plato may not have had an actual genius for action (since, as Nietzsche had pointed out, he had failed to establish any lasting state), but he approved the idea that it was a search for will and imperatives rather than a pure search for contemplative knowledge of being which had spurred him on.

The George Circle, then, had understood the right way to read Plato. But whereas they had read Plato in that way in order to admire and imitate him, Kelsen believed that Plato's political will exposed his philosophy of justice as a hypocritical fraud. The ideal of justice was not objective, it was part of Plato's personal quest for power. And this fed into Kelsen's general commitment to a value-free jurisprudence. States should not pursue moral values such as justice because this is a chimera, always standing for the advantage of one group or other; they should be governed instead by the rule of man-made law.

This approach was derived from Kelsen's allegiance to that other famous circle, the Vienna Circle of the logical positivists. Logical positivism held that value judgements were purely irrational. They were essential to choice and action but could not be logically explained. The way to explain them, therefore, was to debunk them, or in the Viennese terms of the time, to psycho-analyse them. Kelsen's second article on Plato was, accordingly, an essay on Platonic love, published in a psycho-analytic journal.[54] And in both articles he sought to explain (and so explain away) the values of Plato's philosophy in terms of Plato's personality structures of guilt, fear and self-justification.

The key which Kelsen offered to Plato's psyche was his passion for homosexual and pederastic (man to boy) love, the same issue considered already in Chapter 3. Kelsen however took a novel tack.[55] He argued that most Athenians approved of pederasty, if at all, only as a peculiar sort of erotic sideshow. Most pederasts, including Socrates, married and had children as they were expected to do. But Plato, unusually, felt nothing but scorn and disgust for the practice of heterosexuality. He must have felt a deep need to justify himself against the uneasy, mocking regard attracted by his practice of living exclusively among men. And it was this psycho-analytic will to impose his own vision on reality that drove his political and metaphysical commitments (though in his last work, the *Laws*, he gave in to convention, banning pederasty as 'against nature' and bad for the state). His theory of justice was at bottom no more than a theory of self-justification, and his theory of truth as the knowledge of (dualist) other-worldly Ideas was an attempt to justify his own escape from the conventions of this world.

Kelsen employed the George Circle account of Platonic will in order to unmask it. He turned the George Circle adoration of Plato into one more mirage which liberals must expose, in the never-ending series of attempts to pass off personal values as political facts. The battle between the idealization of Plato and the exposé of that idealization occurred within England and Anglophone discourse, between Germany and England, and interestingly, particularly within the Viennese discourse of several who would emigrate. The Oxford-born idealist Plato and the George Circle Plato are not, in structural terms, worlds apart: both look up to Plato as a model for political and moral leadership. But the endorsement of existing moral and liberal values in the former case contrasts with the call for the invention of new moral values, deeper and richer than those of existing polities, in the latter. The result is that adherents of the idealist Plato did not find that putting Plato into practice required radical change to existing political structures and norms, whereas adherents of the George Circle Plato were faced with the more difficult choice of seeking drastic means by which a Platonic spiritual and moral renaissance could come about. Correspondingly, even where the English writers turned against Plato, most still retained their faith in Socrates, a contrast which never became thematic in German debates. Appeals to Plato were of course only a single thread in the complicated evolution of English and German thought in this period, thought which responded to changing political circumstances as well as shaping them. But the different ways in which Plato was read and used in the tense years of the 1920s and 1930s do shed light on the terms of debate which were most resonant in divergent polities.

128

Conclusion: the fate of political philosophy

Faced with the contrasting politics growing out of the George Circle fascination with Plato, let alone with the contrast between (say) Jowett and Popper, the reader may back away in despair. If Plato has been claimed by Nazis, by communist workers, and by disenchanted aristocrats alike, what can one possibly conclude about his politics?

Of course, any writing can be abused. As Socrates memorably explains in *Phaedrus* 275d-e, a written text is helpless and silent in the face of being abused, unless its parent is alive and near to defend it. And the richest texts can be, as it were, systematically abused: elements of their thought will always lead in different directions once unpicked from the delicately balanced layers of the text. In Plato's case, the key elements that have been identified are radical measures to attain reactionary ends, all woven into a holistic view of politics. In the modern debate, the deepest challenge to Plato was that of Popper, precisely because he addressed himself to the holistic aspiration. In rejecting it as intrinsically dangerous, however, he missed an aspect of holism which invites further deliberation. To appreciate this, we make a brief excursus to consider earlier interpretations of Plato's politics, in light of which the blinkered nature of the modern debate will be easier to perceive.

Elizabethan to Enlightenment political Platos

That Thomas More's *Utopia* (1516) models itself on Plato's *Republic* (as had Cicero's *De re publica* and other works) is well known. That James I's Lord Chancellor, Sir Francis Bacon, modelled his *New Atlantis* (1629) on the description of Atlantis in Plato's *Critias* may be less familiar; so too the elements of the *Republic* and the *Laws* which pervade *The City of the Sun* (1602-3) by the Italian mystic Tommaso Campanella. These 'utopias' (literally, from the Greek, 'no-places', a term which More coined to mark a problematic distance from the imagined city his dialogue describes) mimic the Platonic ambition to achieve civic unity and harmony by careful legislation and education to instil the right kind of character into the citizens. These works, which still clung to the republican, and Platonic, sense of the frailty and mutability of things of this world (including governments), were followed by James Harrington's *Oceana* (1656) in which Harrington aimed ambitiously to show how a polity could be made perfectly stable by getting the distribution of agrarian property and the distribution of political office and power into balance.

One side of Platonist politics, then, consists in the elaboration of detailed programmes for the education of citizens and the governance of cities, such as in Plato's *Laws*. But Harrington was also involved in a seventeenth-century manner of treating Plato as the master, not of detailed legal design (which the *Republic*, in contrast to the *Laws*, actually eschews), but of understanding and achieving the principles of social harmony. Jonathan Scott has explained how men like Algernon Sidney, Henry Vane, John Milton, Henry Neville and Marchamont Nedham took this aim from Plato (and also, though secondarily, from Aristotle), in articulating the republican vision that animated their support for the foundation of a republic in 1649, its revival in 1659, and (for some of them) in opposing the imposition of Cromwell's Protectorate and the 'restoration' of Charles II in 1660.

Scott argues that the core of this republican approach, as articulated by Sidney, was the achievement of harmony from the natural variety of human abilities and types. Republicans began with natural equality and liberty, but believed that those who were virtuous would (if allowed the liberty) rise to rule in a kind of meritocracy, imposing on themselves the discipline of submission to reason and, through education and legislation, helping others to impose it on themselves. The inner light of moral guidance which Platonic recollection fostered, and which Anglicans and Quakers in their different ways elaborated, would guide the virtuous in achieving political liberty through this task of reconciling different abilities and aims in harmony. Another student of the period has summarized the shape of Platonic politics which thus emerged as its 'holism': a holism of individual character and civic character, and also of attending to the shaping of interactions among the citizens to bring about harmony.[56]

4. The Political Plato

The Platonic element in seventeenth-century republicanism shows that a holistic understanding of politics need not be intrinsically opposed to liberty, as the Popperian attack on Plato assumed. What would decide their opposition or compatibility is, of course, the particular understanding of liberty in question, as well as the relation between theory and practice advanced. English Civil War republicans understood the fostering of virtue and good character as necessary to liberty. In so doing, they drew on a further Platonic-Christian assumption that there is an objective good which human reason can discern. But they drew also on a republican tradition of thinking about politics which was legitimately indebted to Plato's understanding of the indispensability of education to making human animals into citizens, and to the way in which the laws and ethos of a political society will express fundamental values (values which this tradition envisaged as having been imposed by a legendary lawgiver, such as Solon for Athens, Lycurgus for Sparta, and Moses for the Israelites).

Education and legislation, as the solution to the great problem of reconciling individual liberty with civic harmony, was also ascribed to Plato by important political thinkers of the Enlightenment period. Indeed, these reflections show that the Platonic question of 'who should rule' and the Popperian question of 'how to design institutions to control the rulers' are not so far apart as they may seem. Popper criticized Plato by contrasting him with the great liberal constitutional theorists, who had tried to take 'men as they are and laws as they might be' (as Rousseau put it) rather than trying to mould and transform human nature as Plato had done. But these constitutional theorists themselves profoundly admired Plato for having understood the deep interconnections between psyche and polity, desires and laws. In this light, to think about constitutions is not only to think about detailed balancing of powers, but to think about the moral interactions which would be expressed in civic harmony. Reflecting on the 'spirit' expressed by the 'laws' of every polity, Montesquieu bowed to Plato as having understood the fundamental importance of the choice of regime, and the nature of education, for the desires, aspirations and happiness of the citizens. 'Plato', as Montesquieu observed, 'is not afraid to say that no change can be made in music which is not a change in the constitution of the state'.[57] Rousseau, too, honoured Plato as the first to have perceived that the great political problem of making men free and happy was in fact a problem of education; Rousseau's *Emile*, which describes the education of a single boy, is explicitly intended to be equivalent in its nature and aims to Plato's *Republic*, which he called 'the most beautiful educational treatise ever written'.[58] To attack Plato's *Republic* is in this light to attack the entire tradition of thinking about political philosophy.

The fate of political philosophy

To think about political philosophy is necessarily a holistic endeavour, in the sense of involving thought about the way the various elements of society and culture interact. Popper's attack on putting holism into practice missed this dimension of reading the *Republic* as a work of political reflection, not a political blueprint. However, it is true that to welcome something as theory provides no safeguard against dangerous attempts to put it into practice. In the great tradition of political philosophy, virtue is admirable only if it is genuine, and holistic approaches to politics only if they genuinely aim at a common good. But how to tell whether the aims of a would-be political leader are genuine?

This was the heart of Crossman's attack on Plato's dreams 'of a virtuous Right'. Crossman saw that Plato's aims were not malicious; the *Republic* is genuinely intended to promote the happiness of its citizens. The difficulty is that in promulgating such an holistic vision as a political programme, one becomes hostage to the good intentions of those carrying it out, and there is no protection should those intentions turn out to be otherwise. The theory of holism is indispensable for political understanding. But the practice of holism is always dangerous.

This put readers of Plato in the twentieth century in a difficult position. On the level of practice, Plato's politics offers no guaranteed way to distinguish between false (enforced) and true harmony: between civic education and political propaganda. The George Circle emphasis on Plato's own political drive for its part suggested that the level of practice was the appropriate one on which to evaluate Plato. As the quotation from Nietzsche's *Daybreak* showed, this approach linked Plato's purported political founding with his philosophical founding (and foundationalism): Plato sought to impose a political regime just as he sought to impose a regime of moral values. For Montesquieu and Rousseau, such a task could be achieved only by a lawgiver of legendary proportions. Hitler and his followers took that task upon themselves in the political realm, as George had done for his own values in the cultural realm (though for both, the one realm was a key to conquering the other). The question remaining in their catastrophic wake is how to think about the establishment of values, the connection between self-discipline and true liberty, without falling prey to similar efforts again.

This is to say that political philosophy must take the step which Plato never took: that of thinking through how, without recourse to legendary founders (who can be so horribly incarnated by would-be aspirants), the relation between education and value can be resolved within a democratic regime. Plato makes us aware of the dimensions of the problem: that is the value of thinking through his holism, and he shows the value of an holistic method for elaborating standards of criticism. But he did not believe that it could be solved within democracy, viewing democrats as too self-indulgent to impose the rigours of reason and virtue upon themselves. The challenge for political philosophy today is how to have the courage of the convictions of its past combined with the moderation counselled by the distortions of past practice.

But then Plato can have the last word after all, for combining courage and moderation is essential to the Platonic vision of the good polity (see for example *Statesman* 306a-311c), and, in the *Republic*, of a virtuous soul.[59] His solution was a justice which emerged from the practice of self-discipline. Self-fashioning, as examined in Chapters 2 and 3, was necessary, and must be governed by the virtues. The idea of virtue as self-limitation is not one which the Nazis endorsed, though it is true that it too could fall prey to the dream of the 'virtuous right' as easily as any other element of Plato's programme. Nevertheless, if it can be genuinely achieved (a very large 'if', as we have seen), this Platonic wisdom of virtue as self-limitation is needed both within institutions and also in those places where institutions fall short.[60] Liberals are right to insist that political life would be unbearable without institutional limits to power. Plato saw that political life would also be unbearable without rulers wise enough to bear to limit themselves. The practical problem he bequeaths to us today is how to encourage such virtues in rulers democratically chosen, a practice which itself requires that we practise the virtue of moderation ourselves. And the intellectual problem is how to think about the importance of self-control, which he valued, in relation to the values of individual liberty and democracy, which he did not. Plato's critics were right to discern troubling aspects of the *Republic*'s political programme if that were taken as a blueprint for political action. But the wars about this in the twentieth century obscured the deeper aspects of the *Republic* as a way of thinking about political life and personal virtue in the indispensable tradition of political philosophy. In and after 2001, it is this theoretical dimension of the political Plato which remains to be revived.

5

Conclusion

The acutest searcher, the lovingest disciple could never tell
what Platonism was; indeed admirable texts can be quoted on
both sides of every great question, from him.

Ralph Waldo Emerson, *Journals* (1845)

We have met mirror images of Socrates and Plato in this book:
images which have attracted condemnation as well as praise. Socrates as the individual threatening the life of his city; Socrates as the
individual daring to stand up to the injustice of the majority. Plato's
metaphysics as totalitarian imposition of the false objectivity of the
Forms; Plato's metaphysics as the aspiration to love and beauty,
revealing the Forms in the beauty of the world around us. The
Republic as prototype of a totalitarian state; the *Republic* as model
of the installation of justice in the city and in the soul.

These are not superficial tensions. Each pair arises from deep
aspects of the philosophical world of the dialogues. They cannot be
neatly divided between Socrates and Plato without difficulty: 'Socrates', Plato's Socrates, is the spokesman for all of them. All evoke
in the reader a desire to comprehend, to comprehend the greater
whole within which these could be understood as complementarities
rather than contradictions. And as the dialogues themselves say, to
understand the complex unity of likeness and unlikeness is to learn,
and love, to do philosophy.

The argument of the last chapter can be generalized to apply to
all three sets of oppositions. It is the holistic nature of Plato's vision,
and the holistic situation of Socrates in his trial and death, which
generate these astonishingly contradictory interpretations. By insisting on seeing the structure of the polity as a whole, in which
psychology, economics, emotions and the arts all combine to give a

135

city its character, Plato offered a comprehensive moral analysis which also dictates an imposing, all-embracing political programme. By insisting on the way the Forms give meaning and identity to individual objects and relations, he opened the door simultaneously to immanentist and transcendental readings. And by dying at the behest of Athens for crimes he was accused of committing against it, Socrates simultaneously embodied loyalty to the city as well as opposition to it.

This explains the availability of Plato and Socrates on both sides of most major political and philosophical arguments, as long ago noted by Emerson. But one has still to understand why one side or the other flourishes in particular historical contexts. This book has argued that in the modern period, the driving explanatory force for this has been the need to come to intellectual and political terms with the rise of democracy and the decline in the common public authority of Christianity, both in the context of the morbid modern preoccupation with origins. The effects of hostility to democracy and defence of it on the portrayal of Plato and Socrates have been made sufficiently clear in the preceding chapters. Something further can be said here with respect to religion.

The Victorian institution of Plato as a kind of secular scripture, mentioned in the Introduction, contrasts with the Nietszchean treatment of Plato's philosophy as a kind of original sin, inducing a Fall into false metaphysical abstraction and objectification. Although Nietzsche himself argued that Platonism had been largely superseded by Christianity, the fascination with origins – and the intellectual onslaught on Christianity – have put Platonism in place of the latter as philosophical culprit *par excellence*. In declaring that 'God is dead', Nietzsche seems to have encouraged efforts to revive Plato to fill His place. In this way the moderns have secured railings for their thought (Platonic metaphysics) even while they rail against them. Thus we find in the modern period the extreme views of Plato as the new gospel, on the one hand, with Plato as the initiator of original sin in philosophy or politics: Plato (or Socrates) as (proto-) Christ, versus Plato as Lucifer. Indeed, the strange inflation of Plato to the status of metaphysical or political Prime Source has a whiff of religious superstition about it: as if Plato's supposed malign influence were something he could automatically and magically execute, in the manner of a god. The temptation to force Plato into a straitjacket the better to argue against him bears the mark of repetition of centuries in which philosophers have had to wrestle with the divine.

It is against such absolutizing appropriations of Plato and Socrates that this book has argued. The readings of Plato as a dualist, as a foundationalist, as a totalitarian, as a traitor to Socrates are not without support in his work and what we know of his context. But they share that support with the alternatives they would attack and obscure: Plato as an immanentist, as aspirational in ethics, as theorist of civic structure and education, as teacher of Socrates. To recover these latter readings is, at the start of the twenty-first century, to reopen richer possibilities for appreciating Plato in the round.

And this brings us to the question the reader may be longing to ask: what *should* Plato and Socrates mean for us today? In one sense, of course, that is a question this book cannot answer: it has not set out to engage Plato's texts in the direct critical scrutiny which such an answer would require. The immediate and ultimate response must be that a book of this kind should, in recounting why and how the study of Plato has mattered, encourage readers to study Plato for themselves.

Nevertheless the burden of the answer sketched in the preceding pages is clear. Plato and Socrates should stand for intellectual and political complexity: for the whole of the problem which the one studied, and the other dramatized in his life and death – the problem of how the individual and his or her philosophy stands in relation to the demands of the city and the assumptions of the culture. Attempts to freeze either Plato or Socrates as villain or hero, standing for one answer or another to this problem, hide the deepest thing they can teach us: concern with the problem as a whole in itself. And the fantasy of Plato as quasi-divine, as exercising powerful sway over our imaginations from his grave, makes this worse, by seeming to impose Plato's own answers (or what we take them to be) upon us if we so much as consider them. The American philosopher Jeremy Waldron has summed this up in the way that his students of politics become obsessed with the question of 'what Plato would allow'.[1] They treat the *Republic* as if it were a blueprint put forward for action today rather than a skilled evocation of the complicated issues and ideals involved in thinking about politics in ancient Athens, and, to that extent, anywhere else. And they are resistant to the thought that reading Plato could teach us how to think without automatically controlling what we choose to do.[2]

The approach of this book is intended as an antidote to such superstitious thinking and silly habits of reading. Not only can Plato not mean anything, or have any effect, except through what living individuals do with him, but further, the evidence of the past is that what they do do with him, and learn from him, is astonishingly varied. 'What Plato would allow' is not the right question: we need to understand what we take him to allow, and why.

This leads us to ask of the material already presented, not only how Plato and Socrates have been used, but what has been learned from them. What has been learned from Socrates is both straight-forward and perplexingly obscure. Socrates provides the model of someone devoted to philosophy, who asked incessantly how best to live, though we cannot be sure whether he believed that he had the answers; someone who died loyal to the behest of his democratic homeland, though we can never be sure whether he was loyal to it in his life and teachings. The historical distance between Socrates and us seems easily to evaporate; even the most determinedly historicist readings, situating Socrates as an ancient Greek among other ancient Greeks, end up suggesting parallels between him and our own day. Because Socrates at once fascinated and perplexed his immediate contemporaries, their testimony about him has created a picture which will not cease fascinating and perplexing so long as it is read. The result has been a sense that Socrates is at once too close to us and too remote. As much as one would like to push him away, to consign him to the benighted history of reason or metaphysics, his astonishing powers of innovation and self-definition bring him uncomfortably back.

Socrates could be said to have taught self-fashioning in ethics, and dialogical questioning and the search for definitions as the method of philosophy. Plato's *Republic* has taught the relationship between self-fashioning and civic fashioning: the relationship, as classically put in that text, between soul and city. It raises the question of the whole in politics and ethics: how soul and city reciprocally shape one another. Jean-Jacques Rousseau captured something essential about the *Republic* when he wrote that it was not to be considered solely as a work of political philosophy, but as the greatest work of educational philosophy ever written: the *Republic*, and Plato's works as a whole in their mysterious relation to the real life of Socrates, cannot but teach the connections between psychology and politics, however one evaluates them. And along with other works by Plato, the *Republic* also raises the question of the whole in metaphysics and aesthetics: how, if at all, the particulars of the sensible world reveal what is in some sense transcendent and universal, or in other words, how love connects human longing to what might be called the divine.

The fact that Plato wrote dialogues means that his readers must forever puzzle over what, if anything, his writings were intended to teach. As worlds in themselves, the Platonic dialogues teach us what it is to inhabit a world of thought, a world in which the wholeness of the world is put in question, even while the life of Socrates teaches us something (if we could only understand it) of the difficulty and vulnerability of thinkers who reflect on their polity even as they inhabit it. Viewed over the last two centuries, in light of the characteristic preoccupations of the modern age, the power of philosophy continues to be carried out and carried forward by Plato's work and by Socrates' example. Socrates as a model of self-reflection and conversation, Plato as a model of responding to and going beyond one's teacher. Not the least significant way to understand our fascination with Socrates and Plato is to understand it as an allegory of our desire to teach and to learn, and to understand what those words mean.

Notes

1. Introduction

1. The case was Evans v. Romer. John Finnis (Oxford), a devout Roman Catholic, defends his arguments for the state in 'Law, Morality, and "Sexual Orientation" ', *Notre Dame Law Review* 69, 5 (1994) 1049-76; Martha Nussbaum defends hers for the other side in 'Platonic Love and Colorado Law: the Relevance of Ancient Greek Norms to Modern Sexual Controversies', *Virginia Law Review* 80 (1994) 1515-651. Part of the state's implicit aim was to show that its view of 'public morality' could claim independent philosophical support, and was not based only on sectarian (e.g. Christian) religious views, which would invalidate it under the federal constitution.

2. A.N. Whitehead, *Process and Reality* [Gifford Lectures, 1927-8], edited by D.R. Griffin and D.W. Sherburne (The Free Press, 1978) 39.

3. See p. 143 n. 16 below.

4. Renaissance monks: e.g. George Gemistus Plethon, a Greek based at Mistra, on whom see J. Hankins, *Plato in the Italian Renaissance*, 2 vols (E.J. Brill, 1990) vol. I, Part 2; Victorian students: see L. Dowling, *Hellenism and Homosexuality in Victorian Oxford* (Cornell, 1994), esp. 67, 128-30; Cambridge don: the unpublished manuscript by G. Lowes Dickinson, 'A Dialogue [on homosexuality]', in his Papers, Modern Archives Centre, King's College Cambridge: see p. 147 n. 37.

5. A. Momigliano, 'George Grote and the Study of Greek History' [1952], in A. Momigliano, *Studies on Modern Scholarship*, edited by G.W. Bowersock and T.J. Cornell (University of California, 1994) 15-31, p. 23.

6. The phrase, and the argument here and in the rest of the paragraph, derive from F.M. Turner, 'Why the Greeks and not the Romans in Victorian Britain?', in G.W. Clarke (ed.) *Rediscovering Hellenism: The Hellenic Inheritance and the English Imagination* (Cambridge, 1989) 61-81.

7. J. Glucker, 'Plato in England: the Nineteenth Century and After', in

H. Funke (ed.) *Utopie und Tradition: Platons Lehre vom Staat in der Moderne* (Königshausen & Neumann, 1987) 149-210, p. 191.

8. I owe these points to conversation and correspondence with Susan James.

9. J.J. Winckelmann, *Reflections on the Painting and Sculpture of the Greeks* [1755], tr. H. Fussell (Routledge/Thoemmes Press, 1999) 2.

2. Who Was Socrates?

1. F.D.E. Schleiermacher, 'On the Worth of Socrates as a Philosopher', translated by C. Thirlwall, *Philological Museum* 2 (1833) 538-55, pp. 546-7. The question of whether Plato's writings give us an independently valid portrait of Socrates is still debated today. Compare the defence of this view by G. Vlastos, *Socrates: Ironist and Moral Philosopher* (Cambridge, 1991), with the argument by C. Kahn, *Plato and the Socratic Dialogue* (Cambridge, 1996) that 'Socrates' in Plato's dialogues is a Platonic creation through and through (with the exception, p. 97, of Plato's *Apology*).

2. Aeschines, 'The speech against Timarchus' [345 BCE], in *The Speeches of Aeschines*, with translation by C.D. Adams (Harvard, 1958) 1-157, sec. 173, p. 139.

3. Plutarch, *Lives*, 3 vols, translated by B. Perrin (William Heinemann and Macmillan, 1914) vol. II, 370-3; quoted in Hulse, *The Reputations of Socrates: The Afterlife of a Gadfly* (Peter Lang, 1995) 51.

4. Diogenes Laertius, *Lives of Eminent Philosophers*, 2 vols, with translation by R.D. Hicks (Harvard, 1966) vol. II, 'Socrates', 149-77.

5. Three texts by eighteenth-century savants making this argument are collected in M. Montuori, *De Socrate Iuste Damnato* (J.C. Gieben, 1981).

6. J.J. Hamann, *Socratic Memorabilia* [1759], in J.C. O'Flaherty, *Hamann's Socratic Memorabilia: A Translation and Commentary* (Johns Hopkins, 1967) 167.

7. J.G. Herder, *Ideen zur Philosophie der Geschichte der Menschheit* [1791], edited by M. Bollacher (Deutscher Klassiker Verlag, 1989) 546; as quoted in J.T. Roberts, *Athens on Trial: The Anti-Democratic Tradition in Western Thought* (Princeton, 1994) 210.

8. G. Grote, *Plato and the Other Companions of Sokrates*, 3 vols (John Murray, 1865) vol. I, 6.

9. Grote, *Plato*, vol. I, 251.

10. See M.F. Burnyeat, 'The Past in the Present: Plato as Educator of Nineteenth-Century Britain', in A.O. Rorty (ed.) *Philosophers on Education* (Routledge, 1998) 353-73, pp. 354-62.

11. M. Arnold, *Culture and Anarchy* [1867-69], in *The Complete Prose Works of Matthew Arnold*, V, ed. R.H. Super (University of Michigan, 1965) 85-229, pp. 228-9.

12. Grote, *Plato*, vol. III, 240; quoted in Burnyeat, 'The Past as Educator', 362.

13. M. Alsberg, *Der Prozess des Sokrates* (J. Bensheimer, 1926) 28.

14. K. Popper, *The Open Society and Its Enemies* [1945], 2 vols in one, 4th revised edition (Routledge and Kegan Paul, 1969) vol. I: *The Spell of Plato*, 132.

15. R.H.S. Crossman, *Plato Today* (George Allen and Unwin, 1937) 93.

16. Crossman, *Plato Today*, 300.

17. D. Hume, 'Of the original contract' [1748], in Hume, *Political Essays*, edited by K. Haakonssen (Cambridge, 1994) 186-201, p. 201.

18. The main strategy is exemplified by A.D. Woozley, 'Socrates on Disobeying the Law', in G. Vlastos (ed.) *The Philosophy of Socrates* (Anchor, 1971) 288-318.

19. G. Vlastos, 'Epilogue: Socrates and Vietnam', in G. Vlastos, *Socratic Studies*, edited by M.F. Burnyeat (Cambridge, 1994) 127-33, p. 133.

20. The term is adopted from S. Kofman, *Socrates: Fictions of a Philosopher*, translated by C. Porter (Athlone, 1998) 39, who uses it of Hegel on Socrates only.

21. G.W.F. Hegel, *Vorlesungen über die Philosophie der Weltgeschichte* [1822-3], edited by K.H. Ilting, K. Brehmer and H.N. Seelmann (Felix Meiner Verlag, 1996) 382.

22. Kofman, *Socrates*, 58-9.

23. Nietzsche's many discussions of Socrates are exhaustively analysed in H. Schmidt, *Nietzsche und Sokrates: Philosophische Untersuchungen zu Nietzsches Sokratesbild* (Anton Hain, 1969) where the variations across the different periods of Nietzsche's writings are emphasized, contrary to Walter Kaufmann's account of a consistently positive view of Socrates in *Nietzsche: Philosopher, Psychologist, Antichrist* (Princeton, 1950). See also W. Dannhauser, *Nietzsche's View of Socrates* (Cornell, 1974), still the most comprehensive discussion in English, and A. Nehamas, *The Art of Living: Socratic Reflections from Plato to Foucault* (University of California, 1998), whose elegant meditations in the chapter on Nietzsche have informed the paragraphs here which follow, in particular the final paragraph in this section.

24. F. Nietzsche, *The Birth of Tragedy and Other Writings* [1872], translated by R. Speirs, edited by R. Geuss and R. Speirs (Cambridge, 1999) sec. 13, p. 66.

25. Nietzsche, *The Birth of Tragedy*, sec. 15, p. 74.

26. Nietzsche, *The Birth of Tragedy*, sec. 16, p. 67.

27. Nietzsche, *Twilight of the Idols* [1889], in *Twilight of the Idols / The Anti-Christ*, translated by R.J. Hollingdale (Penguin, 1999) sec. 12, p. 44.

28. S. Schama, *Citizens: A Chronicle of the French Revolution* (Knopf, 1989) 172.

29. Nietzsche, *A Wanderer and His Shadow* [1880], in *Human, All Too Human*, tr. by R.J. Hollingdale (Cambridge, 1978) sec. 6, p. 304, and sec. 86, p. 332. The passage from *The Gay Science* [1882], for which there is no widely available translation, can be found in Nietzsche, *Sämtliche Werke. Kritische Studienausgabe*, 15 vols, edited by G. Colli and M. Montinari, vol. V (Walter de Gruyter, 1973) 11-320, sec. 340, p. 250.

30. G. Sorel, *Le Procès de Socrate* (Félix Alcan, 1889) 13, 34. Sorel declared, p. 10, that Plato had disfigured Socrates and that Xenophon offered the only reliable evidence of the latter's life.

31. Sorel, *Le Procès de Socrate*, 233, 238-9.

32. H. Arendt, *On Revolution* (Faber and Faber, 1963) 98; the brief preceding quotations from Arendt are from 'Civil Disobedience' [1969], in her *Crises of the Republic* (Penguin, 1973) 43-82, p. 49.

33. S. Benhabib, 'Judgment and the Moral Foundations of Politics in Hannah Arendt's Thought', in her *Situating the Self: Gender, Community, and Postmodernism in Contemporary Ethics* (Polity, 1992) 121-47.

34. See D.M. Halperin, *Saint Foucault: Towards a Gay Historiography* (Oxford, 1995).

35. M. Foucault, 'Technologies of the self', in L.H. Martin, H. Gutman, and P.H. Hutton (eds), *Technologies of the Self: A Seminar with Michel Foucault* (Tavistock, 1988) 16-49.

36. Foucault, 'Technologies of the self', esp. 19, 26ff.

37. J. Patoçka, *Platon et l'Europe: séminaire privé du semestre d'été 1973*, translated by E. Abrams (Verdier, 1983), 96.

38. Here I draw on the case made by Nehamas, *The Art of Living*, 70-98.

39. F. Schlegel, *Critical Fragments* [1797], in *Friedrich Schlegel's Lucinde and the Fragments*, translated with an introduction by P. Firchow (University of Minnesota, 1971), no. 108, pp. 155-6.

40. S. Kierkegaard, *The Concept of Irony with Continual Reference to Socrates* [1841], translated and edited by H.V. Hong and E.V. Hong (Princeton, 1989) 214.

41. See T. Flynn, 'Foucault as Parrhesiast: His Last Course at the Collège de France', in J. Bernauer and D. Rasmussen (eds) *The Final Foucault* (MIT, 1994) 102-18, who recounts these lectures by Foucault, and

Nehamas, *The Art of Living*, 157-68 and 180-3, who recounts and criticizes this suggestion of Foucault's along the lines of the next sentence above.

42. J. Annas, *Platonic Ethics Old and New* (Cornell, 1999) 25.

43. R.W. Emerson, 'Plato; or, the Philosopher' [1850] in *The Selected Writings of Ralph Waldo Emerson*, edited by B. Atkinson (Modern Library, 1968) 471-98, p. 486.

44. J. Derrida, *The Post Card: From Socrates to Freud and Beyond*, translated by A. Bass (Chicago, 1987).

3. Plato on Forms and Foundations

1. Aristotle, *Metaphysics*, in *The Complete Works of Aristotle: The Revised Oxford Translation*, 2 vols, ed. J. Barnes (Princeton, 1984) II (I.6, 987b1), among other passages: 'Socrates rejected the study of science for ethics. In ethics he was looking for the universal; he was the first to concentrate on definitions. Plato received his instruction and through this approach came to the conclusion that the universal belonged to a different world from the world of sense-perception.'

2. As quoted without further attribution in E. Scarry, *On Beauty and Being Just* (Duckworth, 2000) 51.

3. Annas, *Platonic Ethics Old and New*, argues that the ancient Platonist tradition (specifically, the 'Middle Platonists' who wrote from the first century BCE to the second century CE) understood Plato to be neither (in my terms) dualist nor foundationalist, and develops their alternative views as plausible ways to understand Plato still. This stimulating book is a model for what is attempted here with regard to more recent readings of Plato.

4. Nietzsche, *Nachlass* 1886/87, in *Sämtliche Werke. Kritische Studienausgabe*, 15 vols, edited by G. Colli and M. Montinari, vol. XII (Walter de Gruyter, 1980) 253; quoted from the translation of this passage in *The Will to Power*, translated by W. Kaufmann and R.J. Hollingdale and edited by W. Kaufmann (Random House, 1968) sec. 572, p. 308. Evidence of Nietzsche's views, such as this passage which expresses views amply attested in his published writings, is admissible despite the dubious status of *The Will to Power* as an entity in itself (consisting as it does of a collection of notes and fragments posthumously edited as a book by Nietzsche's sister).

5. Nietzsche, 'What I Owe to the Ancients', *Twilight of the Idols*, 117.

6. Nietzsche, 'Schopenhauer as Educator' [1874], in *Untimely Meditations*, translated by R.J. Hollingdale (Cambridge, 1983) 125-94, p. 140.

7. Now published as M. Heidegger, *Plato's Sophist*, translated by R. Rojcewicz and A. Schuwer (Indiana, 1997).

8. See W. Beierwaltes, '*Epekeina*. A Remark on Heidegger's Reception of Plato', translated by M. Brainard, *Graduate Faculty Philosophy Journal* 17 (1994) 83-99.

9. M. Heidegger, 'Plato's Doctrine of Truth' [1931/32 lectures, published 1940], translated by T. Sheehan, in W. McNeill (ed.) *Pathmarks* (Cambridge, 1998) 155-82. As A.T. Peperzak, *Platonic Transformations: With and After Hegel, Heidegger, and Levinas* (Rowman and Littlefield, 1997) 100, observes, however, Plato's own sentence (*Republic* 508a1-2) treats the light as a positive not negative yoke.

10. As Stanley Rosen comments: 'The attribution of significance or, in Nietzsche's expression, value to the gifts [of Being] is for Heidegger tantamount to the reification and hence forgetting of Being.' S. Rosen, *The Question of Being: A Reversal of Heidegger* (Yale, 1993) 294.

11. 'On the Essence of Ground' [1929] (translated by W. McNeill) is reprinted in *Pathmarks*, 97-135.

12. Peperzak, *Platonic Transformations*, 71.

13. 'Plato's Doctrine of Truth', 179, as translated by Peperzak. Cf. C. Zuckert, *Postmodern Platos: Nietzsche, Heidegger, Gadamer, Strauss, Derrida* (Chicago, 1996) 52.

14. R. Rorty, 'A World without Substances or Essences' [1994], reprinted in his *Philosophy and Social Hope* (Penguin, 1999) 47-71, p. 49.

15. R. Rorty, *Philosophy and the Mirror of Nature* (Blackwell, 1993) 157, emphasis original.

16. M. Dixsaut, 'Introduction', in M. Dixsaut (ed.) *Contre Platon*, vol. I (J. Vrin, 1993) 1-25, p. 20.

17. I. Kant, *Critique of Pure Reason* [1787], translated by N. Kemp Smith (Macmillan, 1989) 308-14, 667.

18. M. Dixsaut, 'Introduction', *Contre Platon*, vol. I, 20.

19. Hegel for his part thought he had gone beyond Kant's cold formalism, but did not think Plato had been able to do so: Aristotle, not Plato, was his guide to the notion of the immanent or concrete universal. 'The Platonic abstraction ... can satisfy us no longer. We must grasp [the] Idea more concretely, more profoundly, since the emptiness, which clings to the Platonic Idea, no longer satisfies the richer philosophical needs of our spirit today.' *Aesthetics: Lectures on Fine Art by G.W.F. Hegel*, trans. T.M. Knox, 2 vols (Oxford: Clarendon Press, 1988) vol. I, 22. Schelling however based his own absolute idealism on a deep appreciation of Plato.

20. This is the same path recommended by V. Goldschmidt, *Platonisme et pensée contemporaine* (Aubier/ Éditions Montaigne, 1970) 260. Note that it differs from the 'Platonism' of twentieth-century mathematicians such as

Frege, who use the term to describe their belief in the real and timeless existence of mathematical objects (as it were, substances).

21. S.T. Coleridge, *Biographia Literaria* [1817], 2 vols, in *Collected Works of Samuel Taylor Coleridge*, vol. VII, edited by J. Engel and W.J. Bate (Princeton, 1983) vol. I, 233. On Coleridge's Platonism, see D. Hedley, *Coleridge, Philosophy, and Religion: 'Aids to Reflection' and the Mirror of the Spirit* (Cambridge, 2000) esp. 33-87.

22. Emerson, 'Plato', 495.

23. Scarry, *On Beauty and Being Just*, 109.

24. Scarry, *On Beauty and Being Just*, 27, cf. 89-90.

25. P.B. Shelley, 'Adonais' [1812] in *Shelley's Adonais: A Critical Edition*, edited by A.D. Knerr (Columbia, 1984) 27-51, stanza 54, p. 50.

26. W.R. Inge, *The Platonic Tradition in English Religious Thought* (Longmans, Green and Company, 1926) 77.

27. O. Wilde, *The Critic as Artist: A Dialogue*, in *Complete Works of Oscar Wilde*, edited by J.G. Foreman, introduction by V. Holland (Collins, 1969) 1009-59, p. 1040.

28. Wilde, *The Critic as Artist*, 1052.

29. T.H. Green, *Lectures on the Philosophy of Kant* [1875-6], in W. Hamilton et. al., *Philosophy of the Unconditioned* (Routledge: Thoemmes Press, 1993) 29.

30. J.H. Muirhead, *The Platonic Tradition in Anglo-Saxon Philosophy* (London [no publisher], 1931), 228, quoting Bernard Bosanquet on Bradley.

31. F.H. Bradley, *Appearance and Reality* [1897] 2nd edition (George Allen and Unwin, 1920) 451.

32. W. Pater, *Plato and Platonism* [1893], 3rd edition (Macmillan, 1934) 120, 125.

33. See R.V. Merrill and R.J. Clements, *Platonism in French Renaissance Poetry* (New York University, 1957).

34. I. Murdoch, *The Fire and the Sun: Why Plato Banished the Artists* (Oxford, 1977) 36, quoted in F. Kerr, *Immortal Longings: Versions of Transcending Humanity* (SPCK, 1997) 72.

35. Wilde's speech at the first criminal prosecution he underwent, quoted in Dowling, *Hellenism and Homosexuality*, 1-2, a book on which this section relies generally.

36. Dowling, *Hellenism and Homosexuality*, 81.

37. Lowes Dickinson, 'A Dialogue [on homosexuality]', in Unpublished writings of G. Lowes Dickinson © The Provost and Scholars of King's College, Cambridge 2001, quoted by permission and lodged in the Modern Archives Centre, King's College, Cambridge, no pagination.

38. L. Irigaray, 'Sorcerer Love: A Reading of Plato, *Symposium*, "Diotima's Speech" ' [1984], in her *An Ethics of Sexual Difference*, translated by C. Burke and G.C. Gill (Athlone, 1993) 20-33, p. 33.

39. Murdoch, 'Art and Eros: A Dialogue about Art', reprinted in *Existentialists and Mystics*, edited by P. Conradi (Chatto and Windus, 1997) 464-95, p. 491.

40. Murdoch, 'Art and Eros', 492.

41. Murdoch, *The Bell* [1973] (Vintage Books [Random House], 1999) 190, 191.

42. S. Weil, *The Notebooks*, 2 vols, translated by A. Wills (Routledge and Kegan Paul, 1956) vol. I, 45.

43. P.E. More, *The Religion of Plato* (Princeton, 1928) 193.

44. Coleridge, *Biographia Literaria*, vol. I, in *Collected Works*, vol. VII, 304.

45. See J. Smith, 'The True Way or Method of Attaining to Divine Knowledge' [1660] in the excellent collection edited by C.A. Patrides, *The Cambridge Platonists* (Edward Arnold, 1969) 128-44.

46. This point is noted by D. Scott, 'Reason, Recollection, and the Cambridge Platonists', in A. Baldwin and S. Hutton (eds) *Platonism in the English Imagination* (Cambridge, 1994) 139-50, esp. pp. 140, 144-7.

47. W. Wordsworth, 'Ode. Intimations of Immortality from Recollections of Early Childhood' [1815], in *Poems, in Two Volumes, and Other Poems, 1800-1807*, ed. J. Curtis (Cornell, 1983) 271-7, p. 273, lines 58-65.

48. H. Cohen, *Ästhetik des reinen Gefühls*, 2 vols (Bruno Cassirer, 1912) vol. I, 245; P. Natorp, *Platons Ideenlehre: Eine Einführung in den Idealismus*, 2nd edn (Felix Meiner, 1921) 151. I owe these and other references to the Marburg School to K.-H. Lembeck, *Platon in Marburg: Platon-Rezeption und Philosophiegeschichtsphilosophie bei Cohen und Natorp* (Königshausen and Neumann, 1994).

49. Rosen, *The Question of Being*, 12 and passim, argues without reference to the neo-Kantians that 'hypothesis' is in fact exactly the right word to capture Socrates' operations with the Ideas in the dialogues.

50. Cohen, 'Platons Ideenlehre und die Mathematik', in Cohen, *Schriften zur Philosophie und Zeitgeschichte*, 2 vols, edited by A. Görland and E. Cassirer (Akademie-Verlag, 1928) vol. I, 336-66, 344.

51. Green, *Lectures on the Philosophy of Kant*, 111.

52. R.L. Nettleship, *Lectures on the Republic of Plato*, edited by Lord Charnwood (Macmillan, 1929), 228.

53. P. Friedländer, *Plato: An Introduction*, translated by H. Meyerhoff (Routledge and Kegan Paul, 1958), 19. On becoming godlike as the aspiration at the heart of Plato's ethics, see Annas, *Platonic Ethics*, 52-71.

54. Quoted in Goldschmidt, *Platonisme*, 257; quoted here from the Loeb edition, *The communings with himself of Marcus Aurelius Antoninus, together with his speeches and sayings*, tr. C.R. Haines (Heinemann, 1916).

4. The Political Plato

1. 'The Platonic and Aristotelian Traditions', unpublished manuscript originally prepared as a talk (undelivered) for the Open University (BBC Radio) in 1978. Owen Collection, box 1, Classics Faculty Library, Cambridge University, quoted by kind permission of Mrs Sally Owen.

2. B. Jowett, *The Republic of Plato translated into English*, 2 vols, 3rd edition (Clarendon Press, 1908) vol. I, 66-7; vol. II, 24-5.

3. C. Stray, *Classics Transformed: Schools, Universities, and Society in England 1830-1960* (Oxford, 1998) 122.

4. Florence Nightingale, letter to Benjamin Jowett of 1 June 1865, quoted in *Dear Miss Nightingale: A Selection of Benjamin Jowett's Letters to Florence Nightingale*, edited by V. Quinn and J. Prest (Oxford, 1987) 58; the quotation at the end of the paragraph is from Nightingale's letter of 10 November 1894, as quoted on p. xxxv. I owe the reference to this book to an article by Myles Burnyeat.

5. Jowett, *Republic*, vol. I, 9.

6. On women and communism, Jowett, *Republic*, vol. I, 81; II, 56. Jowett admitted that Plato was not a believer in liberty, and that he had not attained a clear conception of the individual as 'the synthesis of the universal and the particular' (vol. II, 59, 96). For that cardinal tenet of Oxford Idealism, promising social harmony, Jowett and some of his followers turned to Hegel. See B. Bosanquet, *A Companion to Plato's Republic* (Rivington, Percival and Company, 1895) 123, who agrees with Hegel that 'Plato, so far from being too ideal, was in fact not ideal enough, because he did not find room for individuality, which is an essential element of all that is rational.'

7. Bosanquet, *Companion*, 55.

8. R.L. Nettleship, *Lectures on the Republic of Plato*, edited by Lord Charnwood (Macmillan and Co, 1929) 177-8, remarks in anti-Hegelian terms that 'corporations have no conscience'.

9. J. Harris, 'Platonism, positivism and progressivism: aspects of British sociological thought in the early twentieth century', in E.F. Biagini (ed.) *Citizenship and Community: Liberals, Radicals and Collective Identities in the British Isles, 1865-1931* (Cambridge, 1996) 343-60, pp. 351-4.

10. E. Barker, *Greek Political Theory*, vol. I: *Plato and His Predecessors* (London [no publisher], 1918) 230.

11. G. Lowes Dickinson, *Plato and His Dialogues* (George Allen and Unwin, 1931) 36, 38.

12. Lowes Dickinson, *Plato*, 89. B. Russell, *The Practice and Theory of Bolshevism* (George Allen and Unwin, 1920) 30, observes the parallels between Bolshevik aims and Plato's *Republic* while supposing that the Bolsheviks themselves would regard Plato as nothing other than an 'antiquated *bourgeois*'.

13. R.M. Weaver, *Ideas Have Consequences* [1948] (Midway Reprint, 1976) 50, 119; the reference in the next paragraph is to p. 177. I owe this reference to Michael O'Brien.

14. L. Strauss, *The City and Man* (Chicago, 1964) 138.

15. I have considered Strauss' reading of the *Republic* more fully in M. Lane, 'Plato, Popper, Strauss, and Utopianism: Open Secrets?', *History of Philosophy Quarterly* 16, 2 (1999) 119-42.

16. All the material on France in this paragraph and the next is from P. Vermeren, 'Platon communiste', in S. Douailler, R.-P. Droit and P. Vermeren (eds) *Philosophie, France, XIXe siècle* (Librairie Générale Française, 1994). I owe my knowledge of the Vermeren and related writings to Edward Castleton. On the feminist interest in Plato, compare the women's club founded by the high-minded feminist Sarah Denman in Illinois in 1866, which devoted its second year of meetings to the reading of Plato, but in an atmosphere which treated Plato as a mystical believer rather than a practical politician. See P.R. Anderson, *Platonism in the Midwest* (Temple University Press, 1963) 126-7.

17. The discussion of Ferrari draws on the Preface by S. Douailler and P. Vermeren to J. Ferrari, *Les philosophes salariés* (Payot, 1983).

18. On Stendhal, see Vermeren, *Victor Cousin: Le jeu de la philosophie et de l'état* (Éditions L'Harmattan, 1995) 100.

19. See the discussion of Fitzhugh's article, 'Black Republicanism in Athens', *DeBow's Review* 23 (1857), in J.T. Roberts, *Athens on Trial: The Anti-Democratic Tradition in Western Thought* (Princeton University Press, 1994) 281.

20. The comments about Plato's communism as 'parasitic' and so on are from G. Thomson, *Aeschylus and Athens* (Lawrence and Wishart, 1941) 368; they are quoted in F.M. Cornford, 'The Marxist View of Ancient Philosophy', *The Unwritten Philosophy and Other Essays*, edited by W.K.C. Guthrie (Cambridge University Press, 1950) 117-37, p. 128. I owe the reference to Cornford to Emile Perreau-Saussine.

21. B. Farrington (the historian of the two), *Science and Politics in the*

Ancient World (George Allen and Unwin, 1939) 94, quoted in Cornford, 'Marxist View', 129.

22. Cornford, 'Marxist View', 131; the 1933 lecture is published as 'Plato's Commonwealth', in *The Unwritten Philosophy*, 47-67.

23. Cornford, 'Marxist View', 130.

24. All references in this and the next paragraph are to W. Fite, *The Platonic Legend* (Charles Scribner's Sons, 1934); the quotation is from p. 74.

25. R.H.S. Crossman, *Plato Today* (George Allen and Unwin, 1937) 133. (This and all other quotations are from the first edition unless otherwise specified. The Preface to the second edition (1959) implies that Crossman did not know Fite's book when writing his own.)

26. Crossman, *Plato Today*, 119.

27. Crossman, *Plato Today*, 266.

28. Crossman, *Plato Today*, 268.

29. Crossman cites Hitler's *Mein Kampf*, Bosanquet's *Philosophical Theory of the State*, and Rosenberg's *Myth of the Twentieth Century* as the only references for his chapter on Nazi uses of Plato, despite the voluminous Weimar and Nazi readings of Plato to be discussed below.

30. Popper also indicates Plato's 'holism', by which he means the valuing of individuals only insofar as they serve the social whole. In the conclusion to the present chapter, 'holism' is used in a different way, to denote understanding the interaction of all aspects of a society without prejudice to the question of whether or how such understanding could be used to redesign it.

31. K.R. Popper, *The Open Society and Its Enemies* [1945] 4th rev. ed. (Routledge and Kegan Paul, 1969) vol. I, 165. A strikingly similar charge is made by Fite, *Platonic Legend*, 74, who says that Plato thinks of himself as a painter in a huge atelier, concerned only to achieve a correct rendition of the ideal pattern.

32. Popper, *Open Society*, vol. I, 121.

33. R. Robinson, 'Dr Popper's Defence of Democracy' [1951] in R. Robinson, *Essays in Greek Philosophy* (Oxford, 1969) 74-99, p. 74.

34. J. Wild, 'Plato as an Enemy of Democracy: A Rejoinder', in T. Landon Thorson (ed.) *Plato: Totalitarian or Democrat?* (Prentice-Hall, 1963) 105-28, pp. 109-14, attacks Popper's philosophy of democracy as inadequate relativism.

35. Thorson, 'Introduction', in Thorson (ed.) *Plato: Totalitarian or Democrat?* 1-12, p. 8. Compare J.H. Hallowell, *The Moral Foundations of Democracy* (Chicago, 1954).

36. Nietzsche, *Daybreak* [1887], translated by R.J. Hollingdale, edited by M. Clark and B. Leiter (Cambridge, 1997) sec. 496, p. 495.

37. H. Friedemann, quoted in F.J. Brecht, *Platon und der George-Kreis* (Dieterich'sche Verlagsbuchhandlung, 1929) 51.

38. W. Jaeger, *Paideia: The Ideals of Greek Culture*, 3 vols, translated from the 2nd German edition by G. Highet (Blackwell, 1939), vol. I [1933], p. 304.

39. Jaeger, 'Die griechische Staatsethik im Zeitalter des Plato' [1924], in Jaeger, *Humanistische Reden und Vorträge*, 2nd edition (Walter de Gruyter, 1960) 195-221. For the *'Führer'* reference, see M. Chambers, 'The Historian as Educator: Jaeger on Thucydides', in W.M. Calder III (ed.) *Werner Jaeger Reconsidered* (Scholars Press, 1992) 25-35, pp. 32-3, and on the general call for such a leader, see K. Sontheimer, *Antidemokratisches Denken in der Weimarer Republik* (Deutscher Taschenbuch Verlag, 1968) 214-22.

40. W.M. Calder III, 'Doceat Mortuus Vivos: In Quest of Ulrich von Wilamowitz-Moellendorff', in U. von Wilamowitz-Moellendorff, *Selected Correspondence 1869-1931*, edited by W.M. Calder III (Jovene, 1983) 1-19, p. 18.

41. Brecht, *Platon*, 23, quoting F. Gundolf, *Dichter und Helden*.

42. Friedländer's letter is reprinted with commentary in U. von Wilamowitz-Moellendorff, *Selected Correspondence 1869-1931*, edited by W.M. Calder III (Jovene, 1983) 127-39. It is also described by H.-G. Gadamer, 'Die Wirkung Stefan Georges auf die Wissenschaft', in Gadamer, *Gesammelte Werke* (J.C.B. Mohr [Paul Siebeck], 1993) vol. IX, 261-70, p. 261, recalling and criticizing Gadamer's own youthful closeness to the Circle. Gadamer's own work on Plato is an important element of German developments which requires further critical scrutiny elsewhere.

43. Ignorance of this important movement in Germany too readily leads scholars to mock the Popper line of attack on Plato. J. D'Hondt, for example, in 'Le destin de l'antiplatonisme', in Dixsaut (ed.) *Contre Platon*, vol. II, 197-234, p. 207, says grandly that Hitler and the Nazis were too busy with their own preoccupations to concern themselves about Plato. As this section shows, this is simply false. There seems to be no complete or even substantially complete account of this story. In R. Bambrough's collection, *Plato, Popper, and Politics* (Heffer, 1967) there are some suggestive contemporary allusions, not always where one would by the title of an article expect them. Of the major German studies of Nazi uses of the classics, those of V. Losemann, *Nationalsozialismus und Antike: Studien zur Entwicklung des Faches Alte Geschichte 1933-1945* (Hoffmann und Campe, 1977), and K.

Sontheimer, *Antidemokratisches Denken in der Weimarer Republik* (referred to above) scarcely refer to Plato. B. Näf, *Von Perikles zu Hitler? Die athenische Demokratie und die deutsche Althistorie bis 1945* (Peter Lang, 1986) has a four-page section on interpretations of Plato (pp. 200-3), also without mention of the George Circle readings; L. Canfora, 'Platon im Staatsdenken der Weimarer Republik', in H. Funke (ed.), *Utopie und Tradition: Platons Lehre vom Staat in der Moderne* (Königshausen and Neumann, 1987) 133-48, does mention Bannes, Hildebrandt and Günther in the context of discussing Wilamowitz, Jaeger and others, but fails to explain or explore the thematic elements of the George Circle interpretation of Plato in any detail.

44. K. Hildebrandt, *Der Kampf des Geistes um die Macht*, 1st edition (Bondi, 1933) 2, 7. In the 2nd edition (Walter de Gruyter, 1959) 395, he says that the manuscript was completed in October 1932 and not changed thereafter.

45. Hildebrandt, *Der Kampf*, 1st edition, 396. In the 2nd edition of this work, published virtually unchanged after the war, these two sentences were omitted and replaced by the following: 'That Plato is the founder of eugenics, was known already by the founders of that movement in England and America at the end of the nineteenth century' (2nd edition, 392).

46. J. Wild, *Plato's Modern Enemies and the Theory of Natural Law* (Chicago, 1953) 26.

47. W. Kaufmann, 'The Hegel Myth and Its Method', *Philosophical Review* 60 (1951) 459-86, p. 485.

48. H.F.K. Günther, *Platon als Hüter des Lebens* (J.F. Lehmann, 1928) 42, 11, 20.

49. J. Bannes, *Hitlers Kampf und Platons Staat* (Walter de Gruyter, 1933) 12, 9, 14, 17, 13. This is the title as it appears in the original edition of 1933. Bannes reverses the order of the terms when he refers to it as 'Platons Staat und Hitlers Kampf' in the Preface to his 1935 book, and that is how it appears, for example, in the catalogue of Cambridge University Library.

50. According to Rosenberg, *Der Mythus des 20 Jahrhunderts* (Hoheneichen, 1934) 78, cf. 287-8, Plato had had instinctive racial contempt for the Socratic idea that the virtues could be learned by all.

51. For the school textbooks, see Kaufmann, 'Hegel Myth', 465. E.M. Manasse, *Bücher über Platon*, 2 vols (J.C.B. Mohr [Paul Siebeck], 1957) vol. II, 186, observes that Otto Neurath co-authored two articles in London in 1944 and 1945 about these textbooks, arguing that the Germans must be prevented from making Plato into a hero after the war.

52. Popper would insist years later that he knew the work of neither

Fite nor Kelsen while writing his own, though he acknowledged them as kindred spirits afterwards. M.H. Hacohen, *Karl Popper – The Formative Years, 1902-1945* (Cambridge, 2000) argues that the major Viennese-period influence on Popper's view of Plato was that of his teacher Heinrich Gomperz and the works of the latter's father Theodor Gomperz, whose work on Greece followed the lines of Grote and Mill (149-50); while in New Zealand he had to teach Plato and read more widely (383-424). Discussing Popper on Socrates, Hacohen fails however to note the long English tradition of lionizing Socrates while attacking Plato (424-8).

53. H. Kelsen, 'Die platonische Gerechtigkeit', *Kant-Studien* 38 (1933) 91-117, p. 99.

54. H. Kelsen, 'Die platonische Liebe', *Imago* 19 (1933) 34-98.

55. The argument is summarised in Kelsen, 'Die platonische Gerechtigkeit', 97-8.

56. J. Scott, *Algernon Sidney and the English Republic, 1623-1677* (Cambridge, 1988), esp. 20-9, 190-4. My reflections on More and Harrington were also stimulated by the unpublished dissertation of E.M. Nelson, the 'other student' mentioned in the text, 'The Greek Tradition in English Republican Thought' (2000), deposited in the Seeley Library, Cambridge.

57. Baron C. de S. Montesquieu, *The Spirit of the Laws*, translated and edited by A.M. Cohler, B.C. Miller and H.S. Stone (Cambridge University Press, 1989) Book II, ch. 8, p. 39.

58. J.-J. Rousseau, *Emile, or, On Education*, translated and edited by A. Bloom (Basic Books, 1979) 40.

59. For discussion of the *Statesman* passage, see M.S. Lane, *Method and Politics in Plato's Statesman* (Cambridge, 1998) 171-82.

60. R. Maurer, 'De l'antiplatonisme politico-philosophique moderne' in Dixsaut (ed.) *Contre Platon*, vol. II, 129-54, pp. 152-4, suggests that such 'autolimitation' may now be required by ecological crisis, a kind of challenge which conventional liberal safeguards against corruption and abuse of power cannot meet.

5. Conclusion

1. J. Waldron, 'What Plato Would Allow', in I. Shapiro and J. Wagner DeCew (eds) *Theory and Practice* (*Nomos*, vol. 37) (New York University Press, 1995) 138-78.

2. M.F. Burnyeat, 'Plato', in *Proceedings of the British Academy* for 2000 (forthcoming), argues that Plato is 'good to think with' by adducing a wide range of historical examples.

Further Reading

General

Burnyeat, M.F., 'Plato' (British Academy Master Mind Lecture, 2000), *Proceedings of the British Academy*, 2000 (forthcoming).

Dixsaut, M. (ed.), *Contre Platon*, 2 vols (J. Vrin, 1993 [vol. I], 1995 [vol. II]).

Fine, G. (ed.), *Plato 1: Metaphysics and Epistemology* (Oxford Readings in Philosophy, Oxford University Press, 1999).

—— (ed.), *Plato 2: Ethics, Politics, Religion and the Soul* (Oxford Readings in Philosophy, Oxford University Press, 1999).

Goldschmidt, V., *Platonisme et pensée contemporaine* (Aubier, Éditions Montaigne, 1970).

Grote, G., *Plato and the Other Companions of Sokrates*, 3 vols (John Murray, 1865).

Hankins, J., *Plato in the Italian Renaissance*, 2 vols (E.J. Brill, 1990).

Kahn, C.H., *Plato and the Socratic Dialogue* (Cambridge University Press, 1996).

Kerr, F., *Immortal Longings: Versions of Transcending Humanity* (SPCK, 1997).

Muirhead, J.H., *The Platonic Tradition in Anglo-Saxon Philosophy* (London, 1931).

Novotny, F., *The Posthumous Life of Plato*, translated by J. Fábryová (Academia Prague, 1977).

Nussbaum, M.C., *The Fragility of Goodness: Luck and Ethics in Greek Tragedy and Philosophy* (Cambridge University Press, 1986).

Peperzak, A.T., *Platonic Transformations: With and After Hegel, Heidegger, and Levinas* (Rowman and Littlefield, 1997).

Scruton, R., *Xanthippic Dialogues* (Sinclair-Stevenson, 1993).

Zuckert, C.H., *Postmodern Platos: Nietzsche, Heidegger, Gadamer, Strauss, Derrida* (University of Chicago Press, 1996).

On Socrates

Dannhauser, W., *Nietzsche's View of Socrates* (Cornell University Press, 1974).

Derrida, J., *The Post Card: From Socrates to Freud and Beyond*, translated by A. Bass (University of Chicago Press, 1987).

Ferguson, J. (ed.), *Socrates: A Source Book* (Macmillan for the Open University Press, 1970).

Fitzpatrick, P.J., 'The Legacy of Socrates', in B.S. Gower and M.C. Stokes (eds), *Socratic Questions* (Routledge, 1992) 153-208.

Hulse, J.W., *The Reputations of Socrates: The Afterlife of a Gadfly* (Peter Lang, 1995).

Kofman, S., *Socrates: Fictions of a Philosopher*, translated by C. Porter (Athlone, 1998).

Montuori, M., *De Socrate Iuste Damnato* (J.C. Gieben, 1981).

———, *Socrates: Physiology of a Myth*, translated by J.M.P. and M. Langdale (J.C. Gieben, 1981).

Nehamas, A., *The Art of Living: Socratic Reflections from Plato to Foucault* (University of California Press, 1998).

Renault, M., *The Last of the Wine* (London, Sceptre, 1986 [original publication 1956]).

Schmidt, H.J., *Nietzsche und Sokrates: Philosophische Untersuchungen zu Nietzsches Sokratesbild* (Verlag Anton Hain, 1969).

Stone, I.F., *The Trial of Socrates* (Jonathan Cape, 1988).

Vlastos, G. (ed.), *The Philosophy of Socrates* (Anchor Books [Doubleday], 1971), including his 'Introduction: The Paradox of Socrates', 1-21.

———, *Socrates: Ironist and Moral Philosopher* (Cambridge University Press, 1991).

———, *Socratic Studies*, edited by M.F. Burnyeat (Cambridge University Press, 1994).

Wallach, J.R., 'Plato's Socratic Problem, and Ours', *History of Political Thought* 18 (1997) 377-98.

On Platonic aesthetics, ethics and metaphysics

Annas, J., *Platonic Ethics Old and New* (Cornell University Press, 1999).

Baldwin, A. and Hutton, S. (eds), *Platonism and the English Imagination* (Cambridge University Press, 1994).

Derrida, J., 'Plato's Pharmacy', in *Dissemination*, translated by B. Johnson (Athlone Press, 1981) 61-171.

————, '*Khôra*' in *On the Name*, edited and translated by T. Dutoit (Stanford University Press, 1995).

Inge, W.R., *The Platonic Tradition in English Religious Thought* (Longmans, Green and Co., 1926).

Moravcsik, J. (ed.), *Plato on Beauty, Wisdom, and the Arts* (Rowman and Allanheld, 1982).

————, *Plato and Platonism* (Blackwell, 1992).

Murdoch, I., *Metaphysics as a Guide to Morals* (Penguin, 1993).

————, *Acastos: Two Platonic Dialogues* (Chatto and Windus, 1986), reprinted as 'Art and Eros: A Dialogue about Art' and 'Above the Gods: A Dialogue about Religion' in I. Murdoch, *Existentialists and Mystics*, ed. P. Conradi (Chatto and Windus, 1997) 464-95, 496-531.

Rosen, S., *Hermeneutics as Politics* (Oxford University Press, 1987).

————, *The Quarrel between Philosophy and Poetry* (Routledge, 1988).

————, *The Question of Being: A Reversal of Heidegger* (Yale University Press, 1993).

Scarry, E., *On Beauty and Being Just* (Duckworth, 2000 [1999]).

Tigerstedt, E.N., *The Decline and Fall of the Neoplatonic Interpretation of Plato* (Societas Scientiarum Fennica, 1974).

————, *Interpreting Plato*, Acta Universitas Stockholmiensis 17 (Almquist and Wiksey International, 1977).

Vieillard-Baron, J-L., *Platon et l'idéalisme allemand 1770-1830* (Beauchesne, 1979).

On Platonic politics

Bambrough, R. (ed.), *Plato, Popper and Politics* (Heffer, 1967).

Barker, E., *Greek Political Theory* vol. I: *Plato and His Predecessors* (London, 1918).

Burnyeat, M.F., 'The Past in the Present: Plato as Educator of Nineteenth-Century Britain', in A. Oksenberg Rorty (ed.), *Philosophers on Education* (Routledge, 1998) 353-73.

Butler, E.M., *The Tyranny of Greece over Germany* (Cambridge University Press, 1935).

Glucker, J., 'Plato in England: The Nineteenth Century and After' in H. Funke (ed.), *Utopie und Tradition: Platons Lehre vom Staat in der Moderne* (Würzburg: Königshausen and Neumann, 1987) 149-210.

Havelock, E., 'Plato and the American Constitution', *Harvard Studies in Classical Philology* 93 (1990) 3-24.

Ober, J., *Political Dissent in Democratic Athens* (Princeton University Press, 1998).

Roberts, J., *Athens on Trial: The Anti-Democratic Tradition in Western Thought* (Princeton University Press, 1994).

Thorson, T.L. (ed.), *Plato: Totalitarian or Democrat?* (Prentice-Hall, 1963).

Tuana, N. (ed.), *Feminist Interpretations of Plato* (Pennsylvania State Press, 1994).

Turner, F.M., *The Greek Heritage in Victorian Britain* (Yale University Press, 1981).

Wallach, J.R., *The Platonic Political Art and Postliberal Democracy* (Pennsylvania State University Press, 2000).

Wells, H.G., *A Modern Utopia* [1905], edited by K. Kumar (Everyman, 1994).

Index

Because Plato is discussed on virtually every page of the book, references to him in the Index are limited to his own writings and his appearance as a character in the writings of others.